REILLY

REILLY

written and illustrated by

Mary Rayner

LONDON
VICTOR GOLLANCZ LTD
1987

First published in Great Britain 1987
by Victor Gollancz Ltd,
14 Henrietta Street, London WC2E 8QJ

British Library Cataloguing in Publication Data
Rayner, Mary
  Reilly.
  I. Title
  823'.914[J]   PZ10.3
  ISBN 0-575-04031-9

Photoset in Great Britain by
Rowland Phototypesetting Ltd, Bury St Edmunds, Suffolk
and printed by St Edmundsbury Press Ltd,
Bury St Edmunds, Suffolk

He knows a lawless law that claims no kin
But meet and plunder on and feel no sin—
No matter where they go or where they dwell,
They dally with the winds and laugh at hell.

From *The Tramp* by John Clare

For Adrian

REILLY

1

The cat-flap clicked upward, letting in a sharp draught of cold air. Framed within the opening appeared a black face with a white nose and chin, wide yellow eyes and a set of curving white whiskers. The face stayed where it was, the eyes surveyed the room.

Bella, lying relaxed and sleepy in the armchair by the kitchen fire, turned her head at the sound. At once she was on her feet, her white fur on end, her ears back. She jumped down from the chair and stood rigid, ready to see off the intruder.

Every line of her body said *This is not your ground*.

Blanche had been stretched on the warm lino in front of the fire. She too sat up in alarm, and watched the confrontation.

The stranger returned stare for stare. His glance had taken in the two saucers of cat-food, one still scattered with untouched scraps, and the blue bowl crusted with a white ring where milk had stood for some time, left by cats who had had more than enough already. He looked at the warm glow of the gas fire, at the armchair and at the clean white coats of the two females. This was a place where a cat could be comfortable, no doubt about that. He was ravenously hungry. He came wholly into the room and approached the saucer cautiously.

Bella circled round him, her fur bristling. Her voice rose in a high sing-song warning. Blanche sprang into the chair and miaowed loudly as if to let the household know there was a stranger in the kitchen.

Before long Miss Betty Braithwaite's sensible medium-height heels could be heard clop-clopping along the hall corridor. The fur along Bella's back smoothed; Miss Betty would set things right. The footsteps came nearer, the door-handle turned and she entered, a small woman with thick hair, once chestnut, now the colour of faded string, pinned off her face and neck.

But the stranger did not turn and flee, as Bella had expected. He stayed where he was. As the door opened, his proud tail drooped, his ears went back in fear and he cowered low to the floor. Cat and woman stared at each other in surprise and doubt. The two white cats watched in astonishment as he crawled cautiously towards her, and she bent to fondle his ears.

"It's all right, puss," she said. "I won't hurt you."

He straightened, reassured by the softness of her voice, and looked up into her face. Then he leant his full weight against her legs, rubbing his head sideways against her brown stockings.

"Come here, Joyce," called Betty over her shoulder. "There's a strange cat in the kitchen, he seems desperately hungry, poor thing."

Her sister Joyce hurried into the kitchen. She was a taller version of Betty, with the same thick hair, but hers was cut shorter in a severe style. "Goodness," she said, watching as the cat turned, arching his back, with all four feet on tiptoe and his tail straight into the air with just the very tip curving over, and came back to repeat his routine. Small mews came from him, suggesting a throat harsh with hunger and thirst. He pushed to and fro, turning his face upward imploringly.

"Ah, the poor love, must be a stray," said Miss Betty, and she hurried to the fridge and poured a large saucer of milk. If her back had not been turned she might have seen a look of triumph cross the cat's face, but when she lowered the saucer to the floor his whole frame was trembling with eagerness.

"Just look at that," said Miss Joyce. "He's so thirsty!"

Black head dropped towards white saucer, pink tongue began to lap with a strength and speed that might have made the sisters wonder, and in a few seconds the saucer was empty.

Betty refilled it. Once again the pink tongue emptied it, and the black face with its strikingly marked white nose and chin was raised beseechingly.

"Come on, Tiger, food now," said Miss Joyce, tipping the cat-food on to the saucer.

The visitor made short work of it, while the two white cats watched in silent dismay. The sisters looked at each other over his crouched form as his tongue moved steadily over the saucer in sideways wipes.

"Let him stay, d'you think?" asked Betty.

"No question," said Joyce. "Bella and Blanche won't mind. He'll be company for them. He may have to be fixed if nobody claims him and we keep him," she said, looking thoughtfully at his rear view as he toured the kitchen, tail high, "but that'll be easy, he's a male, he looks like a young cat. Barely fully grown, I'd say, it'll be a simple matter."

And so it was that Reilly moved into Number Eight, Jubilee Road, on a cold night in February, and became the third resident cat (known as Tiger) in the household of the Braithwaite sisters. As for Bella and Blanche, they put up with him; they had little choice. But they minded a great deal. They waited and watched for a chance to get even.

A few weeks later, in the early spring sunshine, Reilly stepped carefully along the high brick wall at the far end of the garden of Number Eight. He had already made the wall his particular walkway.

From here he could see across all the long, thin box-

11

shaped gardens which ran from the backs of the terraced houses as far as the wall. At the front, the houses presented ornate faces to the world, with broad white eyebrows over each upstairs window and a large bay jutting into each tiny front garden, lining the whole length of Jubilee Road with Victorian yellow brick. But at the back, from where Reilly stood, their tattered underwear was showing. What he saw was a jumbled row, some with tacked-on kitchens and bathrooms, others still with their old outdoor privies, now made over into toolsheds and outhouses, their yards scattered with broken flowerpots, rusting swings and unlidded dustbins, and hung with ragged lines of washing.

It was a promising area, thought Reilly, looking at it with approval. He had made a good beginning by taking over Number Eight and making it his base; from now on he would concentrate on expanding his domain.

He picked his way slowly along the wall, down past the back of Number Six. He lifted one white paw and stepped over the bare thorny branches of the climbing rose which lay along the top of the wall behind the next house, Number Four. Time they pruned it, he thought impatiently, soon it would block his way altogether.

He paused to inspect the kitchen of Number Four through the plate glass of the back door. His yellow eyes searched the darkness of the room beyond for the spindly little black tom who lived there, or the ageing Siamese. No sign. Reilly lowered himself on to what he already thought of as his wall, tucked his white paws neatly under his white chest, and crouched in the sun to watch.

After half an hour the cat-flap below the plate glass swung sharply outwards and Ludo the black tom came out, seemingly unaware of Reilly's presence, and sauntered over to the flowerbed. There he scratched at the earth for a moment and then squatted down, his face taking on the inward look that every cat has when relieving itself. As he tilted his face upward, he could not fail to see through his half-closed eyes the black and white shape looming above him on the wall. Barely waiting to finish, he leapt from his crouched position and made for the safety of the cat-flap. A loud clang echoed through the silent gardens.

Reilly blinked. So. The little black cat had surrendered the garden of Number Four, Reilly had needed only to sit and stare. Good. Reilly looked left and right and then felt his way carefully down on to the trellis which divided Number Four from its neighbour Number Six, and leapt to the ground. He went up to the lavender bush by the plate glass door, turned and sprayed it generously with his scent-mark so that there could be no doubt about who was now in charge of this piece of territory. Then, taking a run at the fence, he was away along the wall to Number Two.

Number Two was going to be more of a problem. The inmates had not yet acknowledged Reilly's authority. Reilly sat on the wall and surveyed the garden thoughtfully.

At the back of the house a grey-haired woman flung up the ground-floor sash window and emptied a pot of tea on to the flowerbed below. A loud barking came from within. As well as the tabby she-cat who lived there, there was a

dog at Number Two, a large yellow labrador which Reilly had met a couple of times on his visits to the garden. The dog had been quite rude, most unnecessarily so. Reilly decided to put off any move on Number Two for the present.

He was still sitting on the wall when a boy of about twelve came down the passageway on the far side. Noticing Reilly, he reached up a hand to chuck him under the chin. "Hi Toots," he said.

Reilly drew back. This was no way to address someone of his standing. He wrinkled his nose and bared his teeth slightly in a hiss to teach the boy manners.

"Okay, okay," said the boy, mistaking indignation for fear, "I wouldn't hurt you. I like cats," and he ran on, his heavy boots echoing down the stone flags of the passage.

So I should hope, thought Reilly, watching the short-cropped mouse-brown head bobbing into the distance. He turned to look with pleasure across the long patch of land which lay alongside the passage, between the wall and the next row of houses. Originally a graveyard, long since disused, its elegant eighteenth-century stones had been allowed to lean and collapse, and the one or two rectangular monuments surrounded by iron palings were overgrown with ivy, their inscriptions invisible under the leaves. Ash saplings, seeded from the high trees overhead, were forcing apart the stone edging, and young nettles were springing from the ground close in to the palings where the mower on its annual rough cut of the grass failed to reach.

For a city cat it made a rare expanse of wilderness among the cramped and concreted suburban gardens, although too many dogs went there for Reilly to feel altogether at ease. But at night, when all the dogs were shut in, when there were only the owls to compete for mice and shrews, then Reilly had been able to take it over as a rich hunting ground of his own.

14

A loud *chink chink* from one of the thorn trees in the graveyard interrupted his thoughts, announcing the anxious presence of a blackbird. Reilly suspected that she was rearing a brood in the dense ivy-covered lower branches of the tree. Her alarm call made him sure.

He turned and walked back up along the wall towards the sound. The call became more frequent; she had seen him. A flurry of leaves, and she left the thorn tree to perch in the tall ash beyond. Reilly crouched, ears and whiskers forward, tail twitching from side to side, and measured the distance from the wall to the thorn tree.

He shifted his weight from one haunch to the other to balance himself for a spring, uncertain whether it was not too far to leap from the wall to the thorn with a stationary take-off. If only the jagged rose branches at the back of Number Four were not in the way, he could take a run. To approach the nest from the ground would be too difficult and too obvious. Maybe when the fledglings were learning to fly would be a better time.

He straightened to a sitting position, and made a show of licking his white chest to save face and to conceal his

change of mind from any possible onlooker. As his tongue worked over the dry fur he realised that he was hungry.

Down the alleyway towards him shuffled an old man with a dog on a lead. Reilly paused long enough to register that the dog was a yellow labrador and then with a lightning flick of his tail he was away back along the wall and down into the garden of Number Two.

He raced up the garden path, slipped under the open sash window and found himself standing on the draining board. On it was a plate of half-eaten cat meat, next to a stack of cups and saucers. Reilly gulped down the meat, and was just sniffing at the top of a half-full bottle of milk and wondering how to get it out when the tabby she-cat wandered into the room.

As soon as she caught sight of him, her fur stood on end, her tail went straight up into the air, and she began to advance sideways on rigid legs, her voice rising and falling in a warning chant.

Reilly gave her a yellow stare. He saw that she was young, with a small pointed face. "Cool it, flower," he said. "You didn't really need it, you look great the way you are," and he jumped on to the windowsill and eased himself under the window frame, rubbing his back luxuriously against it as he went.

"See you around," he called, loping up the garden and jumping back on to the wall. He walked with studied grace along it, stealing a glance over his shoulder as he went. The tabby had followed him as far as the garden and, now that the stranger had left her territory, was sitting gazing at him, her paws together and her fur smooth. It was, thought Reilly as he sauntered homewards, really quite pretty fur.

2

Bella and Blanche were curled fatly by the gas fire when Reilly entered the kitchen. Bella opened her eyes.

"We've been fed," she said. "You were late. You'll see there's not much left," and she tucked her face back under her paw and closed her eyes again.

"I didn't want it anyway," said Reilly. "Who's bothered about a few lumps of *Keen-Kat*?" He moved towards the hearth. Neither of the two residents stirred.

"Hey, move over a bit," said Reilly. "Don't take all the fire."

Blanche uncurled herself, stretched elaborately, each paw in turn, and stared at him. "Why should we? It's our fire. You don't belong here and you never will."

"I do now," said Reilly. "Betty and Joyce haven't said I must go. They put out three saucers for us, don't they?"

"*We* are the cats here," said Blanche. "We came together as kittens and we shall stay together. You are only here because *Miss* Betty and *Miss* Joyce are kind-hearted fools who don't know a scrounger when they see one. This country is going to the dogs. There are far too many scroungers about. What we need is some of the good old-fashioned self-help and hard work that we were taught about when we were kittens."

"Hard work!" said Reilly. "I'd like to see you two lining up in the mouse-hunting queue. You haven't done a paw's turn, either of you, since I've known you."

17

"We do," said Blanche. "We earn our keep. We warm the beds by sleeping on them, and we've spent years allowing ourselves to be stroked and talked to at all hours when we'd rather be asleep."

"A she-cat's work is never done," said Bella with a sigh.

"Rubbish," said Reilly rudely.

"And watch how you speak to us, young fellow," said Blanche. "Or I'll tell the whole street about your operation, when you were taken to the vet's."

This was too much. Reilly called the two females every name he could think of, and then turned and went out again through the cat-flap.

Right, he thought to himself, grinding his teeth in rage. I may be a neutered tom, but I am the fiercest and the toughest cat in the street, and I'll blinking well show them who's top cat around here. Who needs sex anyway? Power is what I'm after.

And he was so beside himself that instead of keeping to the top of the wall, as was his habit, he raced down the alleyway, still muttering and growling under his breath.

I am never, ever, going to go hungry or thirsty again, he

said to himself. I am never, ever, going to have to beg for scraps to get a meal, or crouch under a parked car to get away from the wind and the rain. For the first time in my life I've found a house I can stay in, a house where I am a resident cat and where the humans treat me as a cat should be treated, and I'm going to stay there.

By the time I'm through with them, Bella and Blanche are going to be begging me to allow them to stay on. No, better still, they'll be begging to leave. By the time I've finished, the whole of Jubilee Road will be dancing to my tune—cats, people, everybody. It'll be *my* road, just you wait and see. Mine, mine to do what I like with.

It'd take more than those two to get the better of me, he told himself. Didn't I escape death by drowning when I was a kitten?

His heart beat faster as he remembered that terrible day. He had been born towards the end of the previous summer behind a house that was rented by many tenants. There were a lot of cats about, and no one was ever sure who was responsible for the big tortoiseshell which gave birth to four black and white kittens, but one of the lodgers had decided that enough was enough and they must be drowned. There had been disagreement, and shouting. The loud voices frightened Reilly, and he bit the hand that lifted him up. He was dropped with a thud, but was on his feet in a trice and had darted out into the hall. There he had squeezed in behind a dark wooden chest, and no amount of *Kitty, kitty, kitty?* sweet-called up and down the house would make him reveal himself.

Later he had seen a holdall being carried past, from which had come a dreadful mewing, and he had gone out through the front door to freedom and safety as soon as he saw his chance.

There had followed long months through the autumn and winter when he had had to fend for himself as best he could, living off scraps and such beetles and mice as he

19

gradually taught himself to catch, and though always hungry he had grown into an active and well-muscled young cat.

One life gone, said Reilly now to himself, remembering. The next eight I'm going to live to the full. All at once if need be. The life of Reilly. The nine lives of Reilly. Well, eight anyway, all going on at once.

He was still muttering when he found himself at the furthest end of the alley. It opened here on to the main street, and he stopped abruptly. He had never been this far down the hill before, and only a few feet away from him was a slow-moving line of huge red buses and noisy lorries.

He shrank back into the alley, watching them stop and then lurch into motion again, wrinkling up his nose at the evil smells of exhaust fumes and oil; but then, like a clear high note soaring above an almost deafening bass, he caught the faint wafting smell of roasting duck.

Reilly lifted his head and sniffed, ears pricked and whiskers forward, every sense alert. He turned his head first to one side and then to the other, carefully trying to weigh up the strength of the smell. It was hard among all the other overpowering scents to judge where it was coming from, but it seemed stronger to his right.

He turned, and keeping close in to the shop buildings, ran along the pavement. There were many more people here than he was used to seeing, and he kept well out of the way of passing feet and an occasional pram. As each lorry and car came near, he flattened himself against the wall, terrified that at any moment one of the giant vehicles would advance across the paving stones and crush him, but this did not happen, and he kept on, making little dashes from one shop doorway to the next, drawn by the irresistible lure of that smell.

At last he came to an emerald green door. The smell was singing now, loud and clear. Over his head hung a signboard with strange characters upon it. Reilly sat down to wait, curling his tail round his feet.

Shortly the door swung open and several people stepped out into the street, laughing and talking and doing up their overcoats. They did not look down, and Reilly slipped past them, unseen, into the gloom of the interior.

Inside, the room was lit only by the glow of small latticed lanterns fixed to the walls, hung with tassels and intricately carved, but what a sight met Reilly's widening eyes! Here was not merely one dining table for one house, which Reilly's experience up till now would have led him to expect, but table after table stretching the entire length and breadth of the room, each one laid with a clean white cloth and shining knives and forks, ready for the spreading of a feast.

At some the feast had already started, for people were seated round, and moving quickly between the tables were white-coated men deftly handling dish after dish of delicious food. Reilly was almost overcome by the ecstasy of those smells. Not only roast duck, but gently simmering chicken soup, fried pork, steamed fish, prawns coated in crispy batter—it was a paradise for cats.

Reilly pressed himself against the wall under the rack of coats, keeping well out of the way of the hurrying white-coated waiters. In the half dark only his white bib and paws showed, and he crouched unnoticed, the black orbs of his eyes enormous, savouring the marvel of the various scents, and watching the floor beneath the tables with an unwinking stare in the hope of a dropped morsel of food.

At length he could contain himself no longer, and a lifetime spent scavenging made him break his newly-made vow; he let out a small mew of longing. One of the waiters heard it. He swung round, and came towards him. Reilly could not understand the words he spoke—they were in a language he did not know—but there was no mistaking the controlled anger in his voice, and Reilly turned and fled

21

towards the door. It was closed, and Reilly cowered against it. The waiter flung it wide, giving Reilly's hindquarters a powerful kick, so that he landed on the pavement outside in an ungraceful heap.

Reilly picked himself up and made off along the pavement back the way he had come. He ran as fast as he could, dodging the pedestrians and not stopping until he reached the entrance to the alley.

Here he was back in the neighbourhood of Jubilee Road, nearer to base, and he felt safe, but, he thought, that room with the green door is any cat's idea of heaven. I'll get back there, just see if I don't, and get a share of some of that feasting. That's going to be part of my territory too.

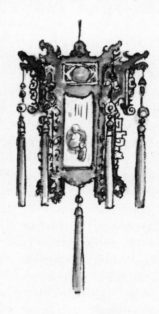

3

In the first-floor bedroom of Number Four, Jubilee Road, Hitachi the Siamese lay curled up under the heavy white counterpane on the big bed, unaware of Reilly's scheming. It was a good place to be, comfortable and warm, and safe from the attentions of young Ludo. Of late Hitachi had found it more and more difficult to manoeuvre himself up under the counterpane, clinging with his long claws to the blanketed precipice of the bed, up on to the plateau at the top, for he was no longer the demon climber that once he had been. A certain stiffness in the joints and an increase in weight made it more of a struggle each day.

Young Ludo was a nuisance. Hitachi would be lying in front of the fire, just dozing off, and Ludo would come skipping up sideways and pounce, aiming disrespectful cuffs at Hitachi's elegant dark ears. Usually the ears would just twitch, and Hitachi would suffer these games, but every now and then he felt it necessary to rouse himself and deal a couple of blows, sometimes pinning the little cat to the floor and giving him a sharp nip.

This had been enough until now to keep Ludo from becoming too cheeky, but sooner or later Hitachi knew that he would have to stand down, and that the little tom would have to be trained to take over, to run the household, pet the humans and keep them up to scratch with their various duties. Someone would have to make sure that the fire was cleared, the coals were carried, the beds made, and the food

bought. And someone would have to succeed to Hitachi's position as the most respected cat in Jubilee Road, the master whose word was law. Was the little cat up to it? Hitachi was not sure.

In all his fifteen years Hitachi had never known the house more chaotic. No one ever sat still long enough for a self-respecting cat to settle on a lap, the front door bell rang ceaselessly with callers whose large feet were a menace if you tried to lie on the floor, noisy machines thumped and howled in every bedroom except Mrs Gooding's, and doors were left open so that icy draughts blew along the hallway and up the stairs. Number Four had never been a warm house, but these days it was uncomfortably cold. For the first time in his life Hitachi regretted his sleek short coat, and wished he had a thick pelt of fur like any common alley cat.

All that was required, Hitachi thought, was a little more warmth, a lot less human yowling, Whiskas on weekdays and chicken liver on Sundays. It wasn't that he wanted a return to the old life, when Mr Gooding had lived with them and Mrs Gooding had been home all day; the children had been something of a trial then. It was just that he wanted a little peace and quiet so that he could retire and live out his remaining years in comfort.

He wondered why the young Goodings needed to make so much noise. I suppose it's the mating season, he thought, but the two girls do seem to have been calling for about four years on end. Cats are much more refined about it, after all, a female cat only calls for a few days every three weeks, not all the time.

Somewhere downstairs a door slammed, footsteps sounded and one of the machines began to churn out a loudly caterwauling human voice. Hitachi shut his eyes and poured himself flat on to the bed in an attempt to sleep. The music rocked and drummed through the house as the volume was turned up.

Hitachi curled tighter, putting a paw over his free ear, flattening it against his head. Why doesn't Mrs Gooding have those three fixed? It would simplify her life enormously, he thought. She grumbles enough about the mess and the racket. The ways of humans are very odd.

Downstairs in Daniel's room Ludo stretched happily and walked towards Dan. He picked his way round the up-turned boots, the piles of discarded clothes and the scattered record sleeves, lifting his paws carefully over the

looping steel traps of broken guitar strings. The boy was lying on his bed—a mattress on the floor—with the music turned up and the curtains drawn. He had just set a match to a forbidden cigarette, and half closed his eyes to draw in the smoke.

Ludo stepped up his chest and laid himself like a black fur collar round the boy's neck. It was a favourite position which Dan had encouraged when he was a kitten. Dan opened his eyes and ran a curving hand along Ludo's spine. Ludo was young. He did not mind the music or the smoke or the half darkness, nor even the warm friendly smell of Dan's fortnight old sheet, and soon his loud purring joined the rhythmic drum-beat and the curlicues of melody outlined round it by the guitar.

In the kitchen the remains of Sunday's chicken on its blue and white china dish stood on the work surface where Dan had left it. Earlier he had made himself what he thought of as a light snack, with a chunk of chicken, a whole tin of potato salad, two slices of bread, some garlic-flavoured cream cheese and two tablespoons of pickle, washed down with a pint of milk and rounded off with a mug of hot chocolate. Now the cat-flap opened gently, and the black and white front half of Reilly lowered itself cautiously into the room.

Seeing that the room was unoccupied, he stepped in over the sill, withdrawing his tail slowly through the flap so that it closed behind him with a faint snick. Through the smell of pickle and garlic he could detect chicken, cream cheese and milk.

He turned and sprang lightly on to the work surface. First he ate the cream cheese. Then he moved towards the chicken. There was enough left to make a satisfying meal, so Reilly crouched down to finish it off. As he ate, a wing piece slipped off the dish and lodged alongside and half under it. Reilly shoved with his nose to reach it, and the big dish slipped sideways and crashed to the floor. Startled,

Reilly leapt to the ground and banged out through the cat-flap.

Once outside he paused and waited. There was no immediate reaction from within the house, the tape was still playing. Reilly attended to the lavender bush again, jumped up on to the wall and trotted homewards.

After his afternoon sleep Hitachi squirmed his way out from under the counterpane and walked to the bedroom door. He limped stiffly down the stairs towards the kitchen, and stopped stock still in the kitchen doorway.

On the floor were the chicken carcass, a scatter of broken pieces of blue and white china, and more fragments of chicken bone and skin. Hitachi came forward and sniffed. There was definitely a smell of cat. Hitachi followed the scent towards the cat-flap, pushed it open and went outside. The pungent smell coming from the lavender bush by the back door made the fur rise along the Siamese's back. He made a tour of the garden but there was no cat to be seen, so he came back into the kitchen and stood with his tail lashing angrily from side to side.

At that moment Daniel wandered into the room, Ludo draped over one shoulder, and took in the scene.

"Hitachi!" he shouted. "You rotten cat, look what you've done!"

He threw Ludo to the floor and made a wild swipe at Hitachi, who dodged and hobbled away up the stairs as fast as his stiff old bones would carry him.

"Oh Hell, Mum will be furious," muttered Dan, crouching down with the dustpan and brush and sweeping up the debris of china and bones. "It can't have been you, Ludo, you were with me."

He stood up, emptied the dustpan, put it down and ran a

desperate hand through his short crop of mouse-brown hair. *"Oh* . . . It was her best dish. What is she going to say?"

Ludo rubbed himself one way and then the other against Dan's ankles, possibly to comfort him but more probably in the hope of a taste of chicken.

"Get away," said Dan, pushing him to one side and striding back towards his room. The door slammed, there was a short silence and then a different, harsher tape echoed through the house, the volume turned up double.

4

Mrs Gooding was not pleased about the dish. Daniel and the two cats were not the only ones affected by Reilly's unseen entry. Dan had waited until after supper to tell her, when his two older sisters, Jane and Anna, had both gone to watch television. He was hoping that the meal would have put her in a mellow mood. He hung about in the kitchen until she had made herself a cup of coffee, but he was out of luck.

"I've a good mind to make you pay for another one," she said, her normally plump and amiable face becoming quite put out when she heard about the accident.

"Why me?" said Daniel, aggrieved. "It was Hitachi."

"You know if you leave food out the cats are likely to try and get it."

"I thought he was too old and stiff to jump that high," muttered Daniel. Then, hoping to make it seem trivial, he made matters worse. "Anyhow, what's an old dish?"

"Oh Dan, it happens to have been a very nice old dish," said his mother wearily. "You can give me half your week's wages from your newspaper round; it won't buy another, but maybe it'll teach you to put things away."

Daniel scowled at her. That would mean another ten days of slavery before he could buy the newly-released record he so badly wanted. He swung out of the kitchen and was on the stairs when she called out after him, "Oh and another thing."

"What?" said Dan.

"Now that you've got that front room you mustn't play your tape-recorder so loudly. I met Mrs Savage at the bottom of the road on my way home and she said she could hear it through her drawing-room window this afternoon, and she's five or six houses up and on the far side of the road."

Dan's face reddened. "That woman! I wish she'd take a long walk off a short pier, somewhere off Australia where there'd be hundreds of sharks!"

"Oh Dan," said his mother, smiling in spite of herself, "but you do play it very loud."

Reilly, tired out by his adventures, had spent the rest of the day sleeping off the cream cheese and chicken on the sofa of Number Six.

Old Mr and Mrs Bayliss who lived there were agreeably friendly. They had neither cats of their own nor children, their three sons having long since left home, and Reilly often visited to sleep on their big squashy rose-covered sofa. In that house the central heating was kept on all day.

"Hallo, Snooky," said Mrs Bayliss, coming into the living room. "How did you get in?"

Reilly had simply shown himself earlier at the double French window at the back, and Mr Bayliss had opened it for him. Mrs Bayliss sat down on the sofa beside him. "How are you den?" And she stroked Reilly's head and back. He was too sleepy to resist, and allowed her to continue, stretching his head upwards so that she could caress his chin and throat. It was not unpleasant, and for an unguarded moment he nearly lost control, feeling his throat beginning to contract and relax into the rhythm of purring. He checked himself. That would be to acknowledge a debt where none existed. Reilly purrs for nobody, he told himself, least of all a human.

"There's my little Snookums," said Mrs Bayliss. "Are you a poor unloved stray den? Doreen Bayliss loves you, don't you worry, my pet." She lowered her face and put it against his fur. Her cheek was dry and soft, and the smell of powder was quite overpowering. Reilly sneezed.

"Really!" said Mrs Bayliss.

No, *Reilly*, thought the cat, why can't she get it right?

"Snooky, pet, I've got to go upstairs for a tick but if you wait there I'll find you some milkie-wilkies."

Reilly winced, and his ears twitched, but he reckoned it was worth putting up with all the soppy talk and the stroking if milk was in the offing. When she had left the room he stood up, arching his back and stretching, and sat waiting for her to return. Then he followed her into the spotless kitchen and watched her open the fridge door and take out a bottle of milk. She poured some into a bowl and set it on the floor. Reilly drank eagerly, at first keeping a wary eye on her, but she stood quite still, just watching, and he soon concentrated wholly on the ice-cold sweetness of the milk, the loop of his tail gradually descending towards the floor as he emptied the bowl.

He watched her return the bottle to the fridge, and caught a glimpse of a cold joint, but although he circled round her ankles mewing in the hope of a morsel of

32

meat, she was too unintelligent to grasp his meaning.

"That's a good puss," she said, stooping to stroke the top of his head, "saying thank you then like a good boy."

Good boy nothing, thought Reilly, deciding no more would be forthcoming from Number Six. He went to the French window and waved his tail about. She should be able to understand *that*, he thought, and sure enough, she came in after him and unlocked the catch.

"Does my little puddy want to go out den?" she said, opening the French window.

Reilly strolled out into the garden in the gathering dusk. He heard the window close behind him, and the clatter of the curtain rings being pulled across. An old garden roller stood by the fence, and he turned and scent-marked it before springing back on to the wall. He might have been unlucky in his visit to the feast-room with the green door, but his takeover of Jubilee Road was going well. First a successful raid on the Ludo household at Number Four, and now bed and board provided if needed at Number Six by Mrs Bayliss. Another willing servant signed up. He was definitely on the way to the top. Number Two next, and a way round the labrador problem.

5

Some weeks later the thick clouds which had covered all the southern half of the country dispersed, allowing the morning sun to shine directly down on to hills and fields, villages and towns. It shone on the city, on slate-tiled roofs and grey pavements, bringing new life to the buddleias rooted in the sides of crumbling chimneys, to the dandelions squeezing up through the pavement cracks, to the worn grass of football pitches and parks. And it shone down on Jubilee Road, with a warmth that had not been felt for many months.

All along one side, along the front of one house after another, the bright beams revealed grime and smears that had gone unnoticed all winter, so that in all the even-numbered houses everyone fell into a flurry of spring-cleaning. In Number Eight Miss Betty and Miss Joyce brought out a stepladder and took down their living-room curtains for cleaning. Next door in Number Six Doreen Bayliss stripped off her rose-patterned sofa and chair covers. Lower down in Number Two the labrador's owner scrubbed the front step till it gleamed. Even in Number Four Dan drew back the curtains in his room and was disconcerted to see a thick layer of dust revealed on his records and tapes.

On the other side of Jubilee Road, on the row of houses facing and exactly matching Dan's row, the odd numbers, the sunlight fell on back walls and yards. There the Chinese families in Number Thirteen hung out line after line of clean washing to dry, and next door in Number Fifteen Mrs Savage sat in her sun-filled kitchen checking her savings and deciding on a new spring suit at a special discount from the Designer Room of the store where she worked.

In the graveyard the ash trees, always the last to come into leaf, held their fattening dark buds out to the warmth, while below them the bluebells sprouted invisible blunt spears in the grass.

At the top of Jubilee Road, where it curved round to meet the end of the alley, the tobacconist cleared away all the out-dated postcards advertising babysitters and used cars from his window. And in the launderette the manageress ran short of coins as every machine swirled and thrummed the winter dust out of curtains and furnishings.

Reilly felt no urge to clean anything. He was sunning himself on the front step of his newly-adopted base at Number Eight when he thought he heard the welcome approaching hum of the milk float, and then the chink of bottles.

He turned his head to look down the road, and there, sure enough, at the furthest end was the milkman coming up the pavement with an armful of bottles. Reilly flowed out and down the pavement in one continuous movement, reaching the milkman just as he walked up the path of Number Two, put the bottles on the doorstep and rang the bell.

Reilly waited, lurking behind the milkman's trousers, and then when the door opened he slipped inside, past the old man who was standing in the doorway. He made his way down the hall towards the kitchen; all the houses in Jubilee Road were built to the same pattern: narrow entrance hall, staircase, two ground-floor rooms off to one side of the hall, kitchen door at the far end behind the stairway.

In the kitchen he crouched under the table. He could smell dog, but there was no sign of the yellow labrador, nor yet of the tabby. He heard the clonk of the bottles being placed on the table above his head, and then saw the old man shuffle back towards the staircase.

Reilly leapt first on to a chair and from there on to the table. He put both paws round a milk bottle and pulled it over sideways. With the force of the fall, milk began to ooze out of the silver-foil top, and as fast as it trickled out Reilly lapped it off the table. When he had had enough he jumped down, and then looked for a way out.

The sash window by the sink was slightly open, enough for a cat to squeeze through.

Reilly slipped through it, and was just emerging when he noticed the yellow labrador lying in the yard, half asleep. Reilly crept on silent paws towards the back wall, belly low

to the ground, but just as he passed it the dog awoke, opened its eyes wide and saw him.

The air was split with frenzied barking, and Reilly shot down the garden towards the wall. He could hear the dog panting just behind him, and then suddenly he felt himself bowled over on to his side. The dog was above him and the sky was blotted out with snarling fangs and yellow eyes. With all his strength Reilly twisted out from under the big paw and sprang for the top of the wall.

The dog hurled itself after him, but it could not reach, and Reilly ran along the top, leaving it standing on its hind legs barking furiously. Behind him Reilly could hear the old man shouting at the labrador, and cursing the spilt milk. "You'll be shut in the front of the house, Goldie, if you can't stop that din. The neighbours will complain."

Reilly slowed, still gasping for breath. Good, if the dog was to be shut in the front that would leave the garden and the kitchen free. There would only be the tabby to confront or—better still—win over. He could see a way to gain entry to Number Two.

He wandered back up the wall towards home, surveying all the other compartments of his gradually expanding kingdom: the gardens of Number Four with its lavender bush, Number Six with its roller, and Number Eight to the right, the disused graveyard to the left. Then, through the gap between the tall trunk of an ash and the rounded mass of the thorn tree, he noticed the tabby she-cat sitting on top of one of the rectangular monuments.

He scrambled down and approached her through the grass, whiskers forward and tail alert. She watched him come, seated motionless on top of the broad stone. Reilly found it impossible to tell whether she was pleased to see him or not. It was certainly easier to approach her off her own territory, and he tried a polite greeting.

She said nothing, but stared at him coolly.

He felt very much at a loss. What could he say to her? Searching for something to win her approval, he said "If you go back home now, you'll find that the milk has been delivered, and you might be given some."

"Oh?" she said. "And why would I need milk now? I can have all I want whenever I want if I ask. Unlike *some* creatures, who take." And she turned away and began to wash her face very delicately with one paw.

Oh goodness, *females*, thought Reilly helplessly. She sounded like Bella and Blanche. There was a long, awkward silence. She was doing behind her ears, making a great show of thoroughness.

"I can show you where there's a nest," he offered.

Her ears came forward and she stopped washing. "Where?"

Reilly took his chance and jumped on to the stone beside her. "Over there," he said, becoming a little more confident. "Wait and watch, and you'll see."

He settled himself on to the stone, placing himself close to her. She did not move away.

For a long time they sat, side by side in the spring sunlight, waiting, both staring at the thorn tree.

This is the life, thought Reilly, the life of Reilly indeed. She was very near, he could almost feel the silky touch of her fur, and her breath smelt sweetly of sardines. Reilly felt

38

his pulse quicken, but he concentrated on the thorn tree, and kept his gaze straight ahead, terrified of turning to meet her eyes in case she should read his thoughts.

"There!" he said.

The hen blackbird swooped down with a beak loaded with grubs, and perched on one of the thorn branches. She cocked her head first this way and that, then with a series of small hops she moved into the thicket of ivy leaves, disappearing from view. A shrill cheeping could be heard.

"Oh!" breathed the tabby. "Brilliant!"

She turned to Reilly, looking at him with enquiry in her face. Reilly felt himself drowning in the green pools that were her eyes, overwhelmed by the headiness of her perfumed breath. With an effort he held still and answered her unspoken question.

"Not yet," he said. "Got to let 'em fatten up. Do the job together, shall we?"

There was admiration in the look she gave him, he was sure. Reilly leapt down from the gravestone, and cantered through the long grass. He made a high curving leap after an imaginary butterfly, and then he danced a hunter's dance for her over the tombstones, with leaps and turns and springs, excitement lending extra power and grace to his limbs. Two humans were coming down the passageway, and he pirouetted on one spot and raced towards them, clearing the low wall beside the footpath with one bound. He scampered round them, and then tore away again down the alley.

The tabby was still watching him, and he rolled over on to his back in the dust, waving his paws in the air and rolling from side to side to show her how pleased he was.

The two humans walked down the alleyway towards him; Reilly had not given them a second glance or seen who they were—all his thoughts were with the tabby. Immediately above him a voice cooed "Oh look, it's Snooky," and Mrs Bayliss stooped down to rub his chest.

Oh Lor', thought Reilly, not her, and he twisted swiftly round to regain his feet and shot off into the long grass.

But the damage was done. "Snooky-wooky," came a shrill call. "Don't run away den, it's your friend, Doreen Bayliss. Come to Doreen. Come on, pet, come on, Snookums."

Reilly ran back to the stone where the tabby was sitting.

"Who's that?" she asked.

"Oh, no one I know," panted Reilly. A look of disbelief, amusement even, crossed the tabby's face.

Reilly could not endure it.

"You're not really called Snooky-wooky, are you? I'm called Francesca." She put her white paws neatly together.

"No I am not! Do I look like a Snooky-wooky?" Reilly's voice came out with raw fury. "My name is Reilly."

"All right, all right, *all right*. I was only asking." Then she walked off, her plumed tail waving, towards the wall. She sprang up and padded along the top towards her home.

Reilly cursed his luck. He would have liked to shout "Come back" after her, but somehow he could not make his voice work fast enough, and in no time the plumed tail had vanished from view as she jumped down into her garden at Number Two.

6

Bella and Blanche were both sitting in the back yard of Number Eight when Reilly returned home at midday.

"Hallo," he said. "Dinner up yet?"

Blanche looked at him. "You never learn, do you," she said. "You're too early this time. And it's called *lunch*."

Reilly walked past her into the house, thinking she might be wrong. He went to look for Miss Betty, and found her folding washing by the airing cupboard on the landing.

He greeted her with a mew and rubbed himself against her ankles, hoping to remind her how near mealtime it was. She went on folding the towel in her hand, but as soon as she had laid it on the pile at her feet she bent to rub behind Reilly's ears. He redoubled his efforts, pushing against her stockinged legs and twisting back and forth, lifting his face and smoothing the side of it hard against her calf.

"There, there," she said. "What's all this about then? You are in a state, aren't you." She picked up the pile of towels and started downstairs. "Come on, Tiger, we'll see what there is for lunch."

Reilly went down in front of her in triumph, tail upright, whiskers jutting, taking care to keep one step ahead. They turned the corner into the kitchen together, and Miss Betty went to the shelf and took down a tin of rabbit-flavoured *Whiskas*, Reilly's favourite.

It was a large tin, and she divided the contents into three portions, put them on three saucers and stooped down to

41

place two of them on the floor. Before she could put down the third, Reilly darted forwards and began to gulp his share down, keeping an eye on the back door.

"Bella? Blanche?" called Miss Betty, going to the back kitchen window. The two white cats stood up and wandered to the back door. Reilly had finished his plateful and was just starting on the second.

"Oh no you don't," said Blanche, seeing him and springing forward to reach her plate. She thrust her white face into the meat, pushing him away.

"Tiger, I'm surprised at you," said Miss Betty.

"I'm not," muttered Blanche, through a mouthful of food. "Absolutely true to type, if you ask me. Can't think why she can't see through him."

But Miss Betty had gone over to the fridge and was lifting out a plate with a cold joint on it. She cut some and arranged a plate of salad for herself. "Here, Tiger, if you're still hungry you can have the bone," and she threw him the large beef bone.

Bella stopped eating and looked across the floor. Her eyes narrowed to slits and she said in a cold voice, "One of these days, Reilly, you're going to get what you deserve. Handsome is as handsome does, that's what I think," and she went back to finishing her *Whiskas*.

Reilly smirked. "You're just jealous," he said. "Silly old sour-puss!"

But Bella went on. "I know what you're up to. Just because you've got Miss Betty under your paw, you think you can rule the whole of Jubilee Road, but you've got another think coming. Wait till you come up against Hitachi at Number Four, he'll tell you how to behave. He's got a pedigree as long as my tail. I warn you, he knows what good manners are, and he won't take any nonsense from you, just you try it. There isn't a cat from here to the top of the hill who can hold a candle to him. *And* he knows a thing or two about fighting."

42

"Oho," jeered Reilly. "Fancied him, did you, in your younger days? That decrepit old thin-coat with the blue eyes! I could knock him into next week any time!"

Bella could take no more. She walked across to Reilly and struck him sharply with one paw across his face.

There was a scrape of a chair and Miss Betty was on her feet. "Bella!" she said. "I gave that to Tiger, you've got your own plateful," and she slapped the white cat, sending her sliding across the lino back towards her saucer. Reilly turned his back, and sniggered into his whiskers.

Blanche said "Watch it, Reilly."

Reilly took no notice but tugged at the remaining scraps of meat on the bone.

"Come on, Blanche," said Bella as soon as they had licked their saucers clean. "We don't have to stay and allow ourselves to be insulted," and the two cats walked out through the kitchen cat-flap and into the garden, where they could be seen carefully washing their faces.

Reilly did not bother to give his whiskers more than a scrape with one paw. Then he climbed into the fireside chair and settled himself for an after-dinner nap.

7

In the Goodings' upstairs sitting room Hitachi and Ludo lay curled together, the larger pale crescent curved round the smaller black ball. The coal fire flamed in the grate, and the dark brown walls glowed in the half light. Daniel's two older sisters were lying flung out on the carpet, their eyes fixed on the television set and *Top of the Pops*.

Daniel was propped on one elbow, watching critically. "Now we get that rubbish video, you'll see," he said. "Can't stand this one," and he leapt to his feet and switched off the set. "Who wants coffee?" He thundered downstairs to make some before the next recording.

Flinging wide the kitchen door in his headlong dash for the kettle, he surprised Reilly, crouched over Hitachi's food bowl, his pink tongue busily polishing it clean.

"Grief," said Dan, "where on earth did you come from?" and he ran at the cat. Reilly fled, crashing through the cat-flap. Daniel waited impatiently for the kettle to boil, poured three mugs full, and went back upstairs. The television was on again.

"There was this black and white cat downstairs," he said. "Either of you seen it before?"

"No," said Anna and Jane, never shifting their eyes from the screen.

"I'll fix it," said Dan, hunching down into the chair with his steaming mug cradled in his hands.

44

Reilly ran home along the wall. Once back in the kitchen of Number Eight he seated himself in his favourite chair and regained his poise by cleaning himself all over. To have been chased out of Number Four was a distinct setback.

Until now he had reckoned that Number Four was virtually won; he had only to look at the little black tom and it ran indoors, and the old Siamese would be easily dealt with, he felt sure, in spite of what Bella had said. But maybe it wasn't going to be quite so easy? He licked himself harder, and had just raised his left back leg to clean between the toes, taking up what Miss Betty called the leg-of-mutton position, when Miss Joyce opened the door and Bella and Blanche walked through.

"There you are, cats," she said. "Goodnight to you," and she shut the door again and went upstairs.

The two white cats gazed unhappily at the cold and colourless gas fire, and looked round the room for somewhere less draughty than the floor. They climbed up on to the two arms of the chair in which Reilly sat, and settled themselves one on either side of him. Bella tried a new approach.

"Going out tonight, are we?" she said, easing herself towards the middle of the chair.

"You're looking pretty good," said Blanche, edging inward from her side. "Pity to waste the evening sitting at home."

Reilly stopped cleaning himself and looked from one to the other in surprise. Compliments from either of them were unexpected. He looked down in pride at his gleaming white chest. It wasn't half bad. He must be looking all right. Maybe it would be worth a visit to Francesca's house? Just a small visit? And maybe even a song outside the back window? Just a quiet, shortish sort of song?

"Might go out a bit later," he said in an offhand way.

With this Bella and Blanche were content, and they settled themselves to wait. Reilly found his eyes closing, and soon all three cats had fallen asleep together in the chair.

About four in the morning Reilly woke. By now Bella and Blanche were lying curled against him, and he eased himself out with care. He crept to the cat-flap and pushed gently with his nose; he had no wish for either of them to find out that he was going visiting. Bella stirred and opened her eyes.

"Where are you off to?" she asked sleepily. "It's very late."

"Sh-sh. Never you mind," whispered Reilly. "Just going out for a little bit of hunting. Won't be long."

Bella changed position, folding her nose underneath her paw. "Bring back a mouse," she said. "You're always on about your hunting, and we've never seen anything you've caught."

Reilly blinked. Didn't they believe him? He felt quite hurt. Thief he might be, but liar he was not, he told himself, not to his own kind.

I'll show her, he thought, his pride wounded, and instead of turning left down the wall towards Francesca's house, he turned right towards the big pairs of Victorian houses up the hill from Jubilee Road. All the large houses

46

up there were divided into bedsitting rooms and flats. Reilly might not know this, but he had swiftly discovered one result, that the gardens behind them were overgrown and untended, and a fine game reserve for mice.

He scurried up the alleyway, passed the launderette and the tobacconist on the corner at the top end of Jubilee Road, and then went on up the next road until he reached the big houses, crossing the road towards them.

He ran through the line of cars parked on the worn grass at the front, past the ranks of dustbins and down the narrow passageway between the two tall pairs of houses towards the back gardens. After the yellow light of the street, the back was dark, and it took him a moment to adjust to the gloom.

When the black orbs of his eyes had widened, he could see what had once been a lawn, a wide meadow of uneven tussocks of grass that had died back over the winter to thick, high, tattered clumps. He settled himself under cover of one of the clumps to wait and watch, sniffing the air for the faintest trace of mouse, and after some while was rewarded by a scent which gradually grew stronger, and then by the sound of rustling in the grass.

The noise came nearer, and Reilly crouched in readiness. The leaves parted a few feet from him, and a mouse scuttled across the gap between that clump and the next. Without a second's hesitation Reilly launched himself into the air and pounced upon it, his jaws closing round the small body before it had even realised the danger.

He took it back through the passageway and allowed himself the game of letting it escape and then springing after it, always making sure to catch it before it could run under one of the parked cars or behind the dustbins. He was busy playing behind one of the cars when Daniel Gooding sped past up the road on his bicycle.

Daniel had dragged himself out of bed at his usual early hour. It was still dark and chill in the bedroom as he struggled into his school trousers and shirt. He ran up the flight of stairs to the bathroom, remembered while in there that his mother had been out late and would be annoyed if woken early, and slowed to walk more quietly down. No time now for a cup of coffee.

He wheeled his bicycle out of the hall, on to the porch and down the front step, and the wind snatched the door and slammed it behind him. Too bad, he thought. He swung out into the road and leaned forward in the saddle to pedal up the hill. The newspaper shop was at the top.

He glanced along a side road as he passed, and saw that one of his school mates, Jonathan, was already half way along it with his canvas bag. When he reached the shop, the last of the piles of papers was being given out by the owner.

Mr Patel frowned. "You are jolly late, Daniel." Daniel, too much out of breath to reply, muttered "sorry" in a gruff voice and took his pile, balancing the canvas bag over his back wheel. The worst day was Sunday, with all the heavy papers to deliver, but today was local paper day, almost as bad, and the bag was bulky with all the house agents' advertisement supplements.

Mr Patel wagged a finger at him. "You deliver to Number Fifteen Jubilee first. The last thing I am wanting is that woman on the telephone again telling me her paper has not come before she is going out to work. And make sure she is

48

getting the local paper properly with its middle pages with all the houses in them."

Daniel scowled, but said nothing. Mrs Savage was a dark cloud in his life. She was bound to report back any mistake he made. She was a professional complainer. There hadn't been any Christmas tip from the Savage house either, he remembered. No silver lining to this cloud.

He turned his bike and freewheeled back down the hill in the dawn light, taking the S-bend of the corner at the top of his road dangerously fast and wide in the sure knowledge that no cars would be out yet. As he turned the wheel out of the first bend, a black and white shape with something in its mouth hurtled across his path.

Daniel swerved, but hit the thing a glancing blow with his wheel. He braked hard, flung the bike down and ran back. From the thump he thought he must have hit its head. There was a black and white cat on the far side of the pavement, sitting looking slightly dazed but not visibly hurt; in the road lay the small corpse of a mouse.

Daniel picked it up by its tail and considered, swinging it gently to and fro. It was quite dead. The cat was by now running away down the hill. Was it the one he had surprised in the kitchen the night before? It seemed to be all right—and if so it didn't deserve its mouse. With a sudden delighted grin he stuffed the mouse in his pocket and ran back to his bike. He propped it against a lamp post and took the papers marked '15'. Then he walked down the deserted road to the house. He took the mouse from his pocket and pushed it through the letter box. There was only the black and white cat, now sitting on the pavement on the far side, who could have seen. Daniel crammed the papers through after the mouse, shoving them well home so that they dropped through inside, and went on with the rest of his round. One present for Mrs S, he thought.

Reilly wanted that mouse, wanted it badly to show Bella. He didn't know where it had gone. His head was hurting

49

and he felt slightly dizzy, but once the boy had finished with the houses on the far side, Reilly crossed over to see if he could find it. He sniffed his way down all the doorways in his search, now and then leaving his scent-mark for good measure, until he came to Number Fifteen. Crouching in the porch with his nose to the bottom of the door, he could smell mouse through the crack. He stood on his hind legs and tried to put his face through the letter box, but it was out of reach, so he sat under the blue estate car and waited.

After half an hour, when still nothing had happened, he moved back into the porch and sprayed it heavily. *That's my mouse*, he thought indignantly, and turned his quarters so as to leave an unmistakable message on the coconut mat as well.

Inside the house, Mrs Savage awoke. Her husband Bill swung himself out of bed and locked himself in the bathroom to shave, while she sipped at the cup of tea provided by the bedside tea-maker. She began to dress slowly, making up with care and combing her dark greying hair into a neat shape. Then she went down to the kitchen.

"Good morning, Ginger Rogers," she said, speaking to the fluffy ginger cat which sat awaiting her. Ginger Rogers was an elegant cat, a cat of great beauty, carefully chosen by Mrs Savage to look good against the olive-gold of the drawing-room carpet and reflect the good taste of her owners. Mrs Savage boiled the kettle, poured milk for the cat, laid the table, and placed two pieces of white slimmer's bread in the toaster. Then she went to fetch the local paper and the *Daily Telegraph*.

The panicky scream that filled the hall brought Bill Savage down the stairs at breakneck speed, razor in hand, his moustache flecked with shaving foam and half his face still white.

"Ginger Rogers, you wretch," she was shouting.

Mr Savage calmed her down and found out from her what had happened. Then picking up Ginger Rogers under one arm, he walked out to the hall, scooped up the mouse and put both out of the front door round by the dustbins.

"All dealt with," he reported back with the understatement of an ex-Army officer, and having completed his shave he settled down to read the *Daily Telegraph*. His wife regained her sense of the rightness and properness of things by going through the local house agents' advertisements, pen in hand, ready to pounce on one for a house on the hill just like theirs, in order to make quite sure that all the Jubilee Road houses were still going up in value.

Ginger Rogers was surprised to find herself dumped by the dustbins with a dead mouse. There was a strong odour of male cat from the front porch, which she found not unpleasant, and as she stood there, looking uncertain, out from under the blue car came a black and white stranger.

"Good morning," he said politely. He had never seen her before but she struck him as extraordinarily beautiful.

There was a pause. "Is this yours?" she asked.

Reilly's mind moved fast. He decided providence would not offer him such an opportunity again. "It *was* mine," he said, "but I delivered it to your house this morning as a present for you."

She looked pleased.

"As a tribute," he improvised. "I have admired you for a long time from across the street."

She acknowledged the compliment with the nod of one well used to such praise. "My name is Ginger Rogers, but the trouble is, I don't very much *like* mouse. I'm not awfully keen on health foods and all this raw goodness, I prefer cooked meat."

"Oh well, in that case," said Reilly, moving forward quickly, "I am sorry to have troubled you. Yes, of course, I should have realised." He regarded her well-brushed coat, the neat velvet flea-collar with the tiny cotton-reel-shaped name-holder hanging from it. She was clearly a cat from a good background, a cat with class. "It was just that I caught

51

it specially for you, it took me all night . . ." his voice trailed away sorrowfully, but he darted swiftly forward and took the mouse in his teeth. He moved back towards the road, turned and began to say something, but found his voice muffled. Ginger Rogers had retreated to the porch.

"Oh dear, how awful for you." She was looking at him with interest.

Reilly put down his burden and said "Can I come and visit you some time? Tomorrow maybe?"

"Oh yes, do," said Ginger Rogers. "I should be delighted."

Reilly took the mouse, crossed the road, tail waving, and ran round to the back door of Number Eight. His head had cleared and he felt tired but triumphant.

He crashed through the back flap, mouse in mouth, and

laid it with a flourish at Bella's feet. "There," he said, stepping back.

Bella gazed at it. Reilly watched her face with satisfaction, then said "Two birds with one stone, in a manner of speaking."

Bella stared at him, mystified. "But it's not a bird, it's a mouse."

"All one to me," said Reilly with a shrug, "but mouse is what you ordered, mouse is what you got."

There was a new respect in Bella's eyes. Blanche climbed down out of the chair and inspected the mouse. The two cats moved to take it back outside and deal with it, but not before Blanche had indicated the armchair to Reilly. "All yours," she said with a bow, "all yours."

8

After breakfast Hilda Savage went upstairs, repainted her mouth, sprayed behind her ears with *Femme* (no sense wasting expensive French scent on Bill at breakfast), and put on her coat and gloves. Bill had let Ginger Rogers back in, and could now be heard trying to start the car. He would drop Hilda at the store where she worked before driving on to his own office.

Mrs Savage turned the front door handle and stood for a moment in the porch, waiting. Only for a moment, but it was long enough. The powerful odour which Reilly had left filled the inside of that sharp, all-in-one-foundationed nose. It swirled up and round her like some evil genie let out of a bottle, attaching itself to her shoes, her skirt, her coat, her hair, smothering the faint, tactful, exotic whisper of *Femme* in an all-powerful, deafening, vernacular shout of *Cat*.

She put the back of her hand across her nose and dived for the front seat.

"Good God, you smell terrible!" exclaimed Mr Savage.

Mrs Savage slipped off her high court shoes and wiped them over with the car leather. "Why on earth . . . ? It can't have been Ginger Rogers, she's female." She was briefly silent as they drove down the road, taking off her gloves. "Only tom-cats leave that smell. It must have been that little black tom-cat of Daniel Gooding's—they're the only people in the road with an un-neutered cat."

Bill's eyes were fixed on the road. Mrs Savage went on, "I'll speak to Mrs Gooding. They'll have to have him operated on. It really is too bad. I mean, it's bad enough having to live next door to the Chinese, drying all their fish at the back, without this at the front."

She sniffed at her gloves with distaste and put them in a plastic bag which was screwed up in the front pocket of the car.

Long years of practice had enabled Bill Savage to sit in a bullet-proof shelter of his own thoughts while the machine-gun rattle of his wife's conversation spattered round him and bounced off harmlessly. He had seen the black and white cat, but he did not much care for cats. Left to himself, he would have liked a dog, but he knew better than to suggest it to Hilda. He could hear the instant hail of bullets: "Muddy pawmarks in the hall"; "Hairs on the drawing-room carpet"; "Dog-food to carry home"; "Exercising it every day".

Now, when she made this statement, he did not bother to put her right, although he knew that a neutered male cat sprays and marks out his territory in the same way as any other. Bill slowed the car as they reached the department store, leaned across and opened the door for her, lighting a cigarette and inhaling with relief as soon as she had gone.

That evening, Mrs Gooding was cooking pancakes for supper when the telephone shrilled. Leaving the pan on its ring, she crossed the room and lifted the receiver, pulling a comic face at her three children, Daniel, Jane and Anna, seated waiting at table. Hilda Savage's voice hurtled into the room. On and on it went, while the underside of the half-cooked pancake curled brownly at the edges and thin smoke began to rise from the pan.

Mrs Gooding tried to break in, but in vain. Dan rose to his feet, and moved across to rescue the pancake. At last the torrent of words stopped.

55

"No, I don't think so," said Mrs Gooding mildly.

The squawk at the other end was so loud that Mrs Gooding held the receiver at arm's length. Finally she was able to say, "I don't think it can be our Ludo, Mrs Savage. He's much too scared of the traffic, he never goes out the front. But look, I'll keep him shut in until a quarter to nine each morning when I leave for work, and then if it happens again we can be sure it wasn't him . . ."

Again she was interrupted, but at last she managed to put the phone down.

She sighed, and crossed towards the stove, repeating Mrs Savage's accusation to the three astonished children.

"Rubbish," said Dan. "Of course it's not Ludo. He wouldn't know how. Much too soppy. Anyhow, he's hooked on me, not other cats. He's a softy, aren't you, Ludo," he said, looking affectionately at the little black cat who lay beside him on the settle. "He's got everything against him; he's black, undersized, scared and gay. Everything the Savages don't like!" and Dan took the second pancake from his mother with a grin.

9

Reilly gave one final lick to his white chest and then walked out of the kitchen of Number Eight. The back door was open to the mild spring air, and hazy afternoon sunlight shone along the top of the back wall and on the lush green of the graveyard beyond. Reilly sprang lightly on to the wall.

Cow parsley foamed around the tombstones, filling the air with sweet scent. He thought briefly and with a slight pang of Francesca, then turned right and uphill along the top of the wall. He reached the end of the row of gardens, and walked round to the road at the front. He crossed with care, and padded down the pavement towards the home of Ginger Rogers. Her house, he told himself, was going to be the next to acknowledge him.

Outside Number Fifteen all was quiet. A few oil puddles darkened the crazy paving of the vacant car lot, the blue estate car was not there. Reilly climbed on to the sill of the bay window and looked inside. He could see Ginger Rogers dozing in the gold velvet button-backed chair in the drawing room. Gently he scratched on the glass to draw her attention.

Her eyes opened. An amber glance at the window and she was on her feet, had jumped down to cross the carpet and come to the window.

"Hallo," she said, "how nice to see you."

"Come out for a walk, it's lovely out," said Reilly.

She looked anxious. "I can't. They've shut me in."

"Why?"

She became embarrassed. "Mummy and Daddy don't like me going out; they don't want me to make unsuitable friends."

"Does that mean me? Stuff Mummy and Daddy," said Reilly cheerfully. "They're just humans—and you mustn't call them that. It's time you found out who your true friends are, petal. One cat's gotta stick up for another. I'll help you get out."

Her eyes opened wide. "You mean *disobey*?"

"Sure thing. Come on girl, where you been all this time? Cats don't do as they're told, cats make their own rules. Obedience is for dogs." He spat out the last word with scorn. "Cats are the only animals humans can't use, hasn't anyone told you that? When'll they be back, this Mummy and Daddy of yours?"

"Gone shopping," said Ginger helplessly. "I don't know."

"Easy," said Reilly. "I'll go back for now, come back when I see their car. No problem. You be ready to come out."

"All right, I will."

Reilly ran back up the road and round to Number Eight. He went in through the kitchen, along the hall passage and into the front room, where he took up a position on the arm of a chair which gave him a clear view of the road outside and the front of Number Fifteen. It was a long wait. He saw several Chinese people return home to Number Thirteen, next door to Ginger's house, but no one came back to Fifteen.

He was still watching when four young Chinese left Number Thirteen about six in the evening, and went down Jubilee Road dressed in the white jackets and trousers of restaurant waiters. A small boy and a round-faced man followed them shortly afterwards.

Dusk was falling by the time the blue estate car drove up the road and turned into the parking space just in front of the house. Reilly raced round and arrived just as Mr and Mrs Savage were unpacking the rear. Their backs were turned, and he was able to see that Ginger was watching through the window. He tried to signal to her to stand by the front door, but she did not understand what he meant, and Mr and Mrs Savage entered the house, slamming the front door behind them.

Reilly jumped on to the sill again.

"Now what?" said Ginger Rogers, looking despairingly through the glass.

"Wait. I'll think of something. The important thing is, if I get them to open that door again, you must be waiting near in the hall so that you can slip out."

"All right," said Ginger. She vanished from view.

Reilly allowed a few minutes to pass and then he took up a threat position; he arched his back, flattened his ears, fluffed up his tail and uttered the terrifying yowls of a fighting cat. For good measure he fixed his eyes on an imaginary foe under the blue estate car, and circled slowly round it towards the front door, his song of hate becoming louder and louder.

He had not long to wait. The front door opened and Mrs Savage came out on to the porch. "There's a cat fight, there

59

must be another cat under the car," she shouted over her shoulder. "Bring the broom!" and she ran back inside having left the door ajar.

"Run for it, Ginger!" shouted Reilly, "here, under the car." He squeezed under and waited, and very soon Ginger was under the car with him, panting with fright and excitement. "Keep still," he ordered, "or they'll see you."

Footsteps came out again, and they could see Bill Savage's feet. The broom was poked under the car and then moved in a wide sweep, but by backing up to the far end they could just keep out of its way.

"Nothing there," said Mr Savage.

"Oh, leave it," said his wife from the porch. "It must have been that wretched little black tom. I'll have to speak to the Goodings again."

"Who are they?" whispered Ginger.

"Shhh. No one you know," said Reilly.

They waited. Mr Savage's footsteps retreated towards the house, and they heard him say with a laugh, "Probably Fred Astaire for Ginger Rogers. Lucky she's shut in," before the front door closed.

"Is that your name?" asked Ginger. "Fred Astaire?"

It sounded a good name to Reilly. "Yeah," he said. "But you can call me Fred. Where'd you like to go?"

"I've never been out after dark," she said. "Do I look all right?"

He looked her up and down.

"Have I got oil on my fur?" she asked anxiously.

"No," he said. "You look fine. Come on."

She giggled. "Mummy and Daddy'll be awfully cross when they find I'm not there."

Reilly gave her a quick look as she trotted after him up the road. He couldn't let her go on calling them that. There was a lot to teach Ginger, but she seemed eager to learn. He thought about it. It was a task he was going to enjoy.

He decided to take her on a tour of his territory. First he led her up the hill towards the tall pairs of Victorian houses with the untended back gardens. They crossed the car-parking area, and Ginger Rogers looked doubtfully at the narrow passageway between the houses, almost blocked by the ranks of dustbins, and at the dark enclosure beyond.

"It's all right," said Reilly. "It's not a trap. We can come and go as we like. I own all this, there aren't any other cats here," and he looked round the enclosure of matted grass and overgrown shrubs with pride. He dropped his voice. "There are *lots* of mice, come, follow me," and he crawled carefully forward.

Ginger tiptoed behind him, looking anxiously to left and right.

"Relax," whispered Reilly. He crouched, and waited. There was a long silence and then he thought he heard a faint rustling. He cocked his ears forward and froze into absolute stillness.

"What are we waiting for?" asked Ginger loudly.

Instantly, at the sound of her mew, something scurried away through the long grass towards the fence. Reilly flung himself after it but he was too late. His outstretched claws

clasped earth and a fistful of grass blades. Whatever it was had got away.

"You fool," he said, turning on Ginger. "You must keep quiet or we'll never catch anything."

"Awfully sorry," said Ginger, and she looked so crest-fallen that he took pity on her.

"Okay. Now watch. Keep still. Don't say anything. Keep quiet."

He moved stealthily towards the far end of the garden, each foot placed carefully after the other, tail switching from side to side. Then he crouched again beside a large bush and waited. There was no sound except the distant throb of a car passing up the hill beyond the houses.

Reilly shifted his position slightly, the pupils of his eyes wide in the dark as he scanned the long grass. Out of the corner of one eye he could see Ginger, sitting watching. After a long wait he thought he caught the faintest sugges-tion of the smell of mouse. He held still. Something was coming out from under the bush. He shifted his weight again, his tail twitched.

The scent grew stronger, and then suddenly beside him a long shaft of yellow light fell across the grass. He turned his head and saw that it came from an oblong of even brighter yellow cut out of the black mass that was the back of the tall house. Ginger saw it too. With a cry of fright she leapt sideways, turned and fled back past the dustbins towards the road. Reilly swore to himself and ran after her.

"Ginger," he shouted. "Wait!"

She slowed down. "What was that?" she panted.

"Only a light being switched on inside the house."

"Oh," said Ginger. "I don't think I want to do any more mouse-hunting, Fred." She shivered. "I don't much like them anyway, I told you."

"All right," said Reilly, disappointed. "I thought you'd like to see how it's done."

"I think I'd better go home," she said.

"No, no, not yet. There's lots more to show you. I haven't shown you the half of it yet. I got lots more places."

He led her down the road towards the graveyard. "There," he said proudly. "That's all mine too. No lights here to frighten you."

She looked at the pale ranks of gravestones, at the glimmer of cow parsley all about them without enthusiasm. "I'm cold," she said. "Haven't you got a house, and a family and a fire? I thought all cats had."

Oh my goodness, thought Reilly, she certainly has a lot to learn. He was silent a moment. Then he said "Yes, of course I have." He thought about Bella and Blanche. "Well . . ." he paused. "I have got a house." He turned his head vaguely in the direction of Number Eight. "But I don't think we'll go there just now. Another time maybe."

She sat down and looked up at the vast dome of the sky overhead. To their left were three small old-fashioned street lights at intervals down the alleyway, casting small round pools of light, but above them, through the tracery of the bare ash branches, the sky was deepest indigo and pierced with stars.

"It's beautiful," breathed Reilly, "don't you think? This is mine. And these trees. And the monuments. They're good for sitting on. And there's a nest in that thorn tree, though all the birds are roosting just now; I'll show you when it's daylight, maybe catch a fledgling." As he said it, the thought of Francesca rose unbidden in his mind. He pushed it to one side.

"Yes," said Ginger with an effort. "Very nice. Thank you for bringing me. Can I go home now? I think Mummy and Daddy may be getting worried . . ."

Reilly interrupted her. "Just look up. Look at the stars. Isn't it marvellous? If you look behind you there's the Great Bear . . ."

She gave a wail and spun round. "Where? What bear? I'm scared, I want to go home."

Reilly gave up. He led her down the alley to the lower end, towards Jubilee Road. Hunting was perhaps not a thing she enjoyed, he would have to try something else. At the foot of the alley the memory of the soaring smell of roast duck came back to him.

"We'll go back now, and I'll make sure your . . ."—he chose the word with care—"*people* let you in, but I'll keep out of sight. In a day or two I'll call round again and take you out to supper. There's a special place I know where they'll do us proud."

10

A few days later Miss Betty returned from the town with a basket of shopping. Miss Joyce was in the kitchen preparing lunch; behind her Bella lay sprawled in front of the fire, while Blanche sat in the armchair watching. Miss Betty put her heavy basket down on the floor, lifted Blanche out of the chair, and sat down wearily. She took out two hairpins where a lock of her hair had come loose, put them in her mouth to free both hands and pushed the disobedient hair back into place.

"I saw Tiger on my way back," she said, "over on the far side of the graveyard, going towards the car park. I called, but he didn't come. He does seem to go much further from the house than Bella and Blanche ever have. D'you think we ought to put a collar on him?"

"I don't hold with putting collars on cats," said Miss Joyce. "They can get caught up on branches and fences. And if you have one of those name-tags they tinkle, and stop them hunting."

"I think it would take more than a name-tag to stop Tiger hunting," said Miss Betty.

"I'll order one this afternoon then," said Miss Joyce. "And a collar with elastic in it, so that if it catches on anything he can get his head out."

Bella nudged Blanche. No one had ever needed to suggest collars for them. Reilly would hate it, but it would serve him right.

A week went by peacefully enough, but then one morning Hitachi was sunning himself in the back garden of Number Four when Reilly wandered along the top of the wall.

Catching sight of Hitachi below him, he halted by the rose and, jumping wide and free so as not to get caught in the branches, landed on the patch of grass below.

The old cat laid back his ears and growled a warning, but Reilly took no notice. Now would be his chance to show Bella's old hero who was master of Jubilee Road. He advanced, stomach low to the ground, each paw deliberately placed; Hitachi backed towards the kitchen door, still growling, his thin tail twitching from side to side. This was his garden and the black and white interloper had no business there. Summoning up all his old fighting spirit he stood his ground.

Reilly came nearer still and then darted forward, boxing left and right at the Siamese's head and ears. The old cat got both his paws round Reilly's neck, and for a wild moment both cats grappled with each other, rolling over sideways, the curving claws of Hitachi's back legs slashing at Reilly's white belly. But Reilly was stronger and younger. He broke free, and before the other could recover, Reilly made a savage slash across his face, opening a deep gash across his left eye.

Hitachi gave a sharp howl of pain and backed away. Sure of victory, Reilly followed, but the old cat had more courage than he realised, and long years of fighting behind him.

Picking the moment when Reilly sprang towards him with his weight on both front paws, Hitachi struck him across his unguarded face. Reilly staggered back in surprise, and Hitachi closed in again, the pain of his own wounded eye making him attack more fiercely.

This was more than Reilly had bargained for. He leapt for the wall and crouched on the top, staring down in silence, keeping his distance.

Hitachi stood below on the gravel, facing Reilly, his tail lashing from side to side. Neither moved, until at length Reilly stood up and walked off down the wall as if he had

just remembered something important he had to do. Then, and only then, did Hitachi go back into the kitchen.

It was some time before the Goodings realised what had happened to their old pet. It was Dan who noticed the swollen face and closed eye when he returned from school, and bathed it with a piece of cotton wool dipped in warm water, but overnight it grew worse, and by next day Hitachi would not be tempted with food. He lay listlessly by the radiator in the kitchen, the whole of the side of his face misshapen and swollen.

"We'll have to get him down to the vet," said Mrs Gooding. "I wonder how it happened? D'you think he walked into something?"

"Mum," said Dan, "he's not that stupid. I've an idea who it might have been," and he told her about finding the black and white cat in the kitchen a week or two back.

"You'll have to walk down to the vet with him in the cat box," said his mother. "I can't be away from work today; I'll ring and make an appointment for you."

That evening when Dan had struggled along the road carrying the heavy cat box the vet was gloomy. Antibiotics could get the swelling down, he said, but Hitachi might have lost the sight of his eye, it was too soon yet to tell. He offered to keep the cat overnight.

Mrs Gooding herself went to fetch Hitachi with Dan the next day. The swelling was a little better but the eye was still bad. "Bring him back in a day or two," suggested the vet, "and we'll have another look at it."

"Poor old Hitachi," said Dan in the car on the way back, poking a finger through one of the air holes in the top of the plastic box, and scratching him softly between the ears. "I could *murder* that black and white fiend."

"We can't be sure," said his mother. "Nobody saw what happened."

They laid Hitachi on a piece of old blanket in front of the radiator. He would not take food, but drank a little milk.

Ludo came skipping into the kitchen, but Dan shooed him out before he could start to torment Hitachi, and closed the door. He sat beside the Siamese and stroked his back gently until he had gone to sleep. Then he wandered out into the garden, idly scuffing the pebbles in the back yard with one plimsoll. His eye fell on a scrap of red leather, and a silver disc, and he stooped to pick it up. It was a broken cat collar, and he read the inscription on the disc: *Tiger*, then a telephone number. Dan breathed in sharply. "And here we have, M'Lud, Exhibit A," he said, imagining the hushed court room, the judge high above him leaning forward to peer over his glasses, as he flourished the broken collar. "A clear case of identification of my client's assailant."

He ran indoors to find his mother.

"Now you've done it," said Blanche.

"Why can't you behave like a civilised feline being?" asked Bella. "Prisoners in our own house!"

Reilly looked from one to the other. Earlier that evening Miss Betty had spoken at some length into the telephone in the hall, and then had come through into the kitchen and gone into the garden. She had returned with a box of earth, put it on the floor and spread newspaper round it. All three cats had watched with growing horror as she wedged a tray against the cat-flap with a chair, so that it could not be opened.

"The indignity!" said Blanche to Bella, rolling her eyes towards Reilly. "Do we have to perform in front of him? Three to a cell?"

"It's all your fault, I heard what Miss Betty was saying," said Bella, turning on him. "And where's your new collar? These things cost money. I suppose you think they grow on trees."

"It wasn't *your* money," said Reilly. "What's it got to do with you?"

"Using this house like a hotel, coming and going at all

hours, expecting food whenever you deign to turn up, never saying where you're going," said Blanche. "*I* don't know," she sighed.

Their voices grew louder and crosser. On and on they went, there was no end to the list of Reilly's misdeeds.

"Oh do shut up," said Reilly, "I want some sleep."

"Oho, *we* want sleep now, do we? D'you expect the whole world to fit in with your sleeping habits, young fellow? Tired after your fighting, is that it? It's all right to go fighting when *we* want to, isn't it," said Blanche sarcastically in a sing-song voice, "now *we* want to sleep, and it's too bad that everyone else has been shut in because of the things *we've* done."

Reilly lost his temper and shouted back. Cat yowls filled the quiet house, reaching such a pitch of fury that none of the three heard Miss Joyce come downstairs in her night-dress, her feet bare. She flung open the door.

"Now then, be quiet. Or there'll be no food tomorrow." She shut the door firmly and went upstairs again.

"I don't care," said Reilly. "I'll go and catch something tomorrow."

"You'll be lucky," said Blanche. "How d'you know the cat-flap will be open tomorrow?"

"Well it certainly won't make any difference to you two if it is," said Reilly. "You couldn't either of you catch a mouse if it was blindfold and on two crutches."

Bella went for him, and there was a short squalling fight, after which all three cats hunched in corners of the room glowering at each other for the rest of the night.

At dawn, woken by the spring chorus of the birds high in the ash trees outside in the graveyard, the cats began again. Miss Joyce came down in dressing-gown and slippers, her face pale with tiredness, her short hair tousled. "I don't think I'm going to be able to cope with this," she said to Miss Betty. "I can't stand another night of this noise."

Miss Betty switched on the kettle to make tea; she gave all

the cats their saucers of morning milk. "We'll see," she said
soothingly to her sister. "Maybe they'll get used to it."

"Used to it nothing," muttered Reilly between laps.

"Shhh," said Miss Betty to him, smoothing the hackles
along his back. "We'll see when the time comes." And she
lifted the chair away from the cat-flap and picked up the
tray.

In the Goodings' house all had been quiet. Hitachi lay on all
through the day by the radiator, still not well. When Dan
and Mrs Gooding drove him to the vet again that evening,
the vet took a careful look at the wounded eye.

"It's no better," he said, "but there is something that
might help, if you can get to John Bell and Croyden in
Wigmore Street in central London tomorrow, and get some
eye drops?"

He lifted Hitachi into the cat box and closed the lid. The
old cat did not try to resist, but hung heavy in his hands.
The vet reached for a pad and pen, and wrote out a
prescription. "Belladonna. It will paralyse the muscles of
the pupil, so that it stays dilated, and will maybe allow the
scratch to heal."

"Oh goodness," said Rose Gooding as they drove home,

71

pushing her hair out of her eyes anxiously. "As if I haven't enough to do over the weekend—I'll have to go into London tomorrow morning."

"You must, Mum. We can't have poor old Hitachi blind," said Dan fiercely.

"Belladonna," said Rose wonderingly. "That's Deadly Nightshade, I'm sure."

"Mum, I don't care what it is, if it makes him better we've got to get it."

11

Reilly trotted down Jubilee Road, his chest gleaming white, his paws spotless, heading for Number Fifteen. When he reached the front of the house, he jumped on to the roof of the blue estate car. From there he could see down into Mrs Savage's drawing room. There were no humans in there, only Ginger Rogers, curled up in the button-backed Victorian chair.

Reilly leapt across on to the windowsill and called through the glass, "Hey Ginger, wake up! I've come to fetch you, I got another place to show you."

Ginger looked up, stretched carefully, first her two front paws side by side out in front of her, chest down low to the carpet, hind quarters high, thick squirrel tail arched over her spine, and then each back leg in turn held stiffly out behind her, toes splayed. "Wait," she said. "I'll be out in a minute."

Then she walked out of the room.

Reilly waited on top of the car, his eyes on the front door. Very soon it opened, and Ginger came through.

"How did you get them to let you out?" he asked. She was improving, he thought.

"Oh, easy," said Ginger with a giggle. "I just squatted down on the gold carpet as if I was going to mess it and Mrs Savage let me out in double quick time."

"Good for you," said Reilly approvingly. "But now I

hope you're hungry because I'm going to take you for a treat."

"Ooh," said Ginger, "where?"

"Follow me," said Reilly, and he walked down Jubilee Road towards the main street.

"Not hunting?" asked Ginger, a note of anxiety in her voice.

"No, no. Something else. You'll like this."

They had reached the main street with its teeming traffic, and Ginger looked about her in alarm. She shrank back against the base of a shop window.

"It's all right," said Reilly. "They don't come up on this bit, they only come up to here," and he showed her where the road ended and became pavement. A huge red bus drew up a few feet away with a squeal of brakes and then waited, the rhythmic throb of its engine making the pavement under their paws tremble. There was a hiss and then a rattle and its doors opened to disgorge several passengers on to the pavement.

Ginger backed away towards Jubilee Road.

Reilly ran after her. "Come on, they're only people. Come with me, you'll be all right, promise."

"Yes," she said obediently. Reilly ran along the street, turning every now and then to make sure she was following. They scurried from doorway to doorway until they reached the emerald green door with its hanging sign. It was firmly shut.

"We have to wait here," said Reilly. From under the door he could distinguish the scents of steamed fish, prawn heads, spare ribs and roast duck, with just a hint of honey and garlic.

Ginger said "I can smell food."

Great, thought Reilly sarcastically, she's coming on, and then at once regretted his unkind thought. But *was* she, perhaps, a little slow? Thick, even? He did not want to admit it to himself, but any cat should have been able to separate out at least two of the smells. Just inexperienced, he told himself. Aloud he said "Yes. Maybe we should try round the back?"

Beyond the building with the green door there was a narrow passageway, almost blocked by a pile of cardboard boxes, and then, past the boxes, a low wall. Reilly and Ginger skirted the boxes and jumped up on to the wall. There were about ten dustbins in a double row by the back door, more cardboard cartons heaped up, and in one of them under a high window, a stack of yellowing cabbage leaves which gave off a sour smell. Ginger wrinkled up her nose as they passed.

The back door was open, and they could see a fat man with a knife in his hand chopping something. The scents of cooking food through the door were stronger now and more promising.

"Do we go in?" asked Ginger.

"No, stay here. They may not be ready for us yet." He made her hide behind the dustbins.

"I thought this was one of your places," said Ginger Rogers.

"Well, not exactly. You'll have to do as I tell you, these are funny people."

Ginger was studying the fat man's profile, his small nose and broad cheeks, the warm gold colour of his skin; he did not look at all like Bill Savage, the only other grown man she knew well. She thought of the sharp outlines of Bill's face from the side, with its tobacco-stained bristly moustache, and of the even sharper little profile of his wife Hilda. She decided that this human looked a whole lot friendlier.

Reilly was crouched beside her behind the bin, trying to work out what to do next. The cook went on chopping. After some time he scooped up all the mushrooms which he had been slicing and dropped them into a large bowl, then carried it through a far door, leaving the room deserted. Reilly led the way forward.

75

He tucked himself under a low bench piled with crates of a green leafy vegetable, well out of sight, and indicated to Ginger that she should follow. But Ginger Rogers sat down in the middle of the room, curled her magnificent yellow-barred tail over her paws and looked about her.

Reilly could hear footsteps returning towards the far door. "Ginger!" he hissed, but he was too late. He watched, paralysed, as the cook re-entered the room. He could not fail to see her. But to Reilly's amazement the cook's round Chinese face broke into an enormous smile, and he bent to stroke her. He said something in a strange language, and called out over his shoulder. A woman padded into the room, scooped up Ginger and carried her in her arms through the door into the inner room of the restaurant.

Reilly drew back under the bench and kept hidden. Why had they been so pleased? It was very mysterious.

A small boy came into the room and said something. Reilly could not understand the words. The man patted the jet-black head of straight hair affectionately, and spoke in

reply. There was a little more conversation, and then the boy said with a broad smile in English, "Very lucky. Ginger cat."

A waiter came out into the scullery with a tray of dirty dishes. The little boy took a bowl and collected a pile of spare rib bones off the dirty dishes, and then, holding it carefully out in front of him with one hand, opened the far door with the other and disappeared into the inner restaurant.

Reilly waited under his bench while the fat cook's legs moved about the kitchen. He crouched until the legs went out of the far door again, and then the small boy came back into the room, this time empty-handed. Now was his chance, Reilly thought, to try *his* fortune.

He came out from under the bench and advanced cautiously towards the boy.

The boy saw him. He shouted, and reached for a meat cleaver. There were no English words this time. It did not take a second for Reilly to decide that this was not a welcome.

He leapt for the high window, skidded down outside in an avalanche of cartons and rotting cabbage leaves, slid across a dustbin lid and fell with a clatter on his side on the ground. He could see the boy coming after him through the back door, the cleaver in his hand.

Forgetting all possible concern for Ginger, Reilly ran as fast as he could along the street in the dark until he reached the alley. He careered round the corner and flattened himself against the wall out of sight. After a minute he peeped back round to see if he was still being followed. There were several people walking along the pavement but he could see no sign of the Chinese boy.

He sighed with relief and walked back up the alley. He felt badly shaken up and now began to wonder what would happen to Ginger. He hopped up on to one of the rectangular monuments and sat there, cleaning himself all over from

head to tail in order to soothe his shattered pride. Then he tucked his white paws under his chest and sat for a long while, contemplating in the dusk.

Inside Number Eight Miss Joyce and Miss Betty were washing up the supper things together.

"I don't know where Tiger is," said Miss Betty.

"No," said Miss Joyce. "Bella and Blanche are in the front room but I haven't seen Tiger since this afternoon."

"Shall we shut them in again tonight, d'you think?"

"If they make a noise like last night I won't be able to stand it, Goodings or no Goodings," said Miss Joyce.

Miss Betty looked thoughtful, "We'd better give it a try."

"You go and call Tiger out the front. I'll try the back."
Miss Joyce went out into the back garden. "Tiger, Tiger,
Tiger?" she called, her voice rising in a chant. "Oh Tiger,
where are you? Come on, food time." She whistled for him
as if he had been a dog. "Tiger!"

At the front Miss Betty was doing the same. In Jubilee
Road all was quiet. Miss Betty stopped calling and paused
to listen; she could hear no cat, only the faint sound of Miss
Joyce calling behind her over towards the graveyard. And
then from further away she could hear someone else calling. She listened more keenly; faintly, rising from behind
the houses facing her, and slightly higher up the hill, she
could hear an echoing voice. "Ginger, Ginger, Ginger? Oh
Ginger, where are you? Come on, food time. Ginger!"

What a coincidence, Mrs Savage, thought Betty, but she
did not wish to be caught in one of Mrs Savage's webs of
woe, so she dodged indoors again as fast as she could
before Mrs Savage should come out into Jubilee Road and
look there.

Reilly sat on his plinth of stone, an immoveable sphinx, and
turned his ear towards Miss Joyce's calling voice. He had no
desire to be locked in again all night. He decided to stay
where he was and say nothing.

Suddenly there was a mew and a shadowy form came up
out of the dark on to the monument beside him. It was
Francesca.

"Hallo," she said. "Who's being called? There's a right
to-do tonight. People calling all over. Who's missing?"

Reilly was too tired to be anything but honest with her.
"Well, me," he said unhappily, and explained about the
locked cat-flap the previous night.

"Oh," she said. "Do they call you Tiger?"

"Yeah."

"How odd, you're not even striped." She paused, and

considered her own delicately marked paws. "And what happened to the golden-furred friend I saw you with last week?" There was a slight edge to her voice.

"Gone," said Reilly, and he recounted the escapade in the Chinese restaurant.

"Dear, dear," said Francesca. "Sounds to me as if she's all right, though. So you didn't get any food? And you're going to be locked in? You'd better come home with me and I'll smuggle you in for a snack. Or better still, we could go hunting together."

"I don't really feel up to hunting, Francesca, if you don't mind."

"All right," said Francesca. "I'll fix something for you. You can call me Fran if you like, most people do," and she led him back down the alley towards the rear of Number Two.

The kitchen window was open at the bottom, and the two cats slipped in.

"Stay there," said Francesca. "I have to check where Goldie is," and she ran out of the door into the hall. Reilly waited in the dark room until she returned. She said briefly "That's all right, he's asleep; you can have some of his food, he never finishes it."

Reilly ate the chunks of dog-food in quick gulps, one eye on the door.

Fran said "It's all right, you're quite safe for now. But you can't stay, he might come in here."

Reilly finished the plateful, sat back and ran a tongue over his whiskers. He felt a little better. He would have liked to stay with Francesca, but he could probably find shelter for the night in one of the back outhouses or sheds, maybe even in the Bayliss's, he thought; the evening was mild. "I'll be going then," he said awkwardly. "And thanks, Fran." He went out through the window, jumped up on to the wall and was gone.

12

"Mum?" said Dan.

The kitchen table was scattered with the remnants of breakfast. Mrs Gooding's eyes were fixed on the centre pages of Saturday's *Guardian* which was spread across the table. She did not look up. "Mmm?"

Anna and Jane sat side by side on the settle, hunched over the quick crossword. "I know," said Anna in triumph, "look, that's what it must be," and she pencilled in a word.

"*Mum*," said Dan, more urgently. He was standing behind her chair, holding his cricket boots. "I don't think Hitachi is any better, he's still lying down all the time. *Please* can you go and get this eye stuff? And the other thing is, it's Jonathan's party this evening and my birthday next week and what would you say if I dyed my hair?"

"I know," she said, taking in only part of his question. "What would you like to do for your birthday?"

"I'd like to go to the Chinese Restaurant, all of us, we've never been, and perhaps Jonathan too."

"Oh, yes," said Anna, all attention suddenly, "do let's."

Mrs Gooding considered. "Good idea. I think I can run to it. Next Saturday, say?"

"Great," said Dan, "that's okay then," and he strode out of the kitchen. In the silence that followed, the final words of his question echoed in Mrs Gooding's mind. What had he said about dying his hair?

"What colour?" she shouted after him.

"It's okay, Ma," said Jane reassuringly. "I think he's going to do it black, to be like Jonathan."

Outside in Jubilee Road the milk float hummed gently up the hill. Dan swung out of the front door of Number Four and started up the pavement towards Jonathan's house, carrying his cricket things.

"Mornin'," said the milkman. "Your Mum there? She owes three weeks'."

"Yes," said Dan, pausing. The milk float halted and the milkman climbed out. Reilly walked down the road towards them both, his tail waving, and came up to the milk float, putting his front paws on the footboard of the driver's seat and sniffing inquisitively.

"He yours?" asked the milkman. "I thought he lived at Number Two."

"He's from Number Eight," said Dan. "But you want to watch that one, he gets away with murder, he'll be driving your milk float off as soon as you turn your back."

The milkman laughed.

"No really, he acts like he owns the road. He gets fed in every house except ours and everybody's got a different name for him."

"Milkman!" called a shrill voice from higher up the hill. Dan and the milkman exchanged understanding looks.

"Oh Lor'," said the milkman, "what've I done now?"

Mrs Savage was advancing down the road with a piece of paper in one hand and a roll of Sellotape in the other. Dan dodged off up the road, while Mrs Savage wrapped the paper round a lamppost and strapped it in place. Over her shoulder she said to the milkman, "We've lost our cat, she never came home last night, ginger, very pretty. If you see or hear of her will you let me know?"

"Yes, Madam," said the milkman. "I'll be up to your 'ouse in a minute." He pressed the bell of Number Four.

Rose Gooding came out, still in her dressing-gown, saw

Mrs Savage and realised she was trapped. Dan, coming back with Jonathan, had time to cross the road to avoid her. Mrs Savage came up the steps of Number Four. "I've been wanting to have a word with you. It's about the house next door to us, where all the Chinese live."

On the far pavement Dan caught Jonathan by the arm and pulled him to a halt. They stood to listen, concealed by the milk float.

Mrs Savage's voice rang out up and down the street: "There are far too many of them living in that house, that man who owns the Jade Garden, he's got them packed in there like rabbits. I'm going to write to the Council to complain, and if all of us do they'll pay more attention."

"But why?" said Dan's mother. "What harm do they do?"

"Well, my dear, have you thought what will happen to the value of your house with those people opposite?" She lowered her voice. "Of course I wouldn't like you to think I've got anything against them personally, I'm sure they're very nice people; but their ways are different from ours, and they come here and think they can live five and six to a room as if they were still in Hong Kong. It's statutory overcrowding, and I shall say so."

"Oh dear," said Mrs Gooding.

Say something, Mum, willed Dan, don't let her think you agree.

But Mrs Savage went on. "My dear, the smell of their fish drying in the back yard! And so much washing too . . ."

Jonathan pulled at Dan's arm. "Come on."

"Hang on a minute," said Dan. He heard Mrs Savage say, ". . . maybe she's gone looking for your little black one. He's the only un-neutered tom in the road. You should do something about him."

"I'm sorry if you've lost your cat," his mother said stiffly. "If I hear anything I'll let you know," and she gathered her dressing-gown about her and went back into the house.

83

Mrs Savage turned to re-cross the street, and Dan and Jonathan broke into a run downhill towards the main road.

"That woman is too much," said Mrs Gooding to Jane and Anna in the kitchen of Number Four. She sighed, and sat down wearily; then she remembered Hitachi.

She went over to him where he lay on the old blanket, and bent down. He opened one eye and half lifted his head.

"Poor old thing," said Mrs Gooding, running a hand along his flank. He felt hot to her touch. "Heavens, I don't like the feel of him at all, I think he's running a temperature. Oh glory, the vet isn't open again until Monday. I'll go and get dressed and drive up to John Bell and Croyden and get those drops right away. Jane, can you tell Dan I've gone, and see if you can both get Hitachi to take some milk?"

13

Reilly walked up the road ahead of the milk float and round to the back of Number Eight. The cat-flap was open.

"Ah, there you are!" said Miss Betty. "Come on, Tiger, you must be very hungry, come and have a late breakfast," and she tipped a whole big tin of Whiskas on to a dish for him. Reilly had spent the night curled up on the spare bed in the Bayliss's house, and was more thirsty than hungry. He lapped the bowl of water dry and then turned to the food.

"Back again, are we? You had everyone out looking for you last night," said Bella.

"Where were you?" asked Blanche.

Reilly did not pause from his eating to reply. He was tired of their questioning, what business was it of theirs? He finished the dish, then went into the front room and slept a long, replete sleep.

When he awoke he sat on the arm of the chair and looked through the front window at the houses opposite. What had happened to Ginger?

After some while he wandered out again through the cat-flap, avoiding Bella and Blanche, and leapt up on to the wall. He sat with his paws tucked under him and surveyed his territory. First there was the graveyard. Excellent, he thought. Thick with cow parsley and meadow grass now and providing good cover—he must do something about those blackbird fledglings. He closed his eyes, tucked his

paws more firmly under him and allowed himself a little anticipatory daydream in which he captured three or four plump little blackbirds under the admiring gaze of Ginger Rogers. His tail twitched and without meaning to, his mouth opened in the almost soundless yittering of a cat about to close on its prey.

He came to with a jolt, opened his eyes and looked round to make sure that no one had observed him. It would be shaming if they had. There was no one in sight. Nevertheless he cleaned his chest self-consciously, then looked down from the wall at the rest of his domain, along the backs of all the houses in Jubilee Road, and checked them off in his mind.

His adopted home at Number Eight was still his, he considered, in spite of the small matter of the nightly blocking of the cat-flap; Number Six, the Bayliss's, was his; Number Two, where Fran lived, was making good progress—he had ready access; Number Fifteen on the other side of the road, Ginger's house, might not be worth troubling about if Ginger was gone. In all Jubilee Road there was not a single house where he could not come and go as he pleased except for Number Four.

Number Four was, he had to admit, still a problem. It was the one house that had withstood his campaign. The old Siamese had been put out of action, and the undersized black tom would not be too difficult to overcome in a straight fight if that proved necessary, but maybe it wasn't the cats who were the real enemy? There was Dan, Dan the boy. It must have been Dan who had got him and Bella and Blanche shut in at nights. Any visits to Number Four would have to be made when Dan was out of the way, thought Reilly. Anyway, no human being really understands how a cat's mind works, I'll get the better of him. I'll make it all work out somehow, I always do, he told himself, his usual optimism taking over, and he ran down the alleyway to see what had become of Ginger Rogers.

When he reached the Jade Garden he approached cautiously down the side passage past the dustbins. Ginger was sitting in the back yard, cleaning fur that already gleamed. She was no longer wearing the velvet collar, he noticed.

"Hallo, Fred," she said.

Reilly turned his head automatically to look behind him, then remembered and said, as casually as he knew how, "Wotcher!"

She resumed licking the inside of her front leg.

Reilly said urgently, "Come on, why don't you get away now, it'd be easy."

Ginger lifted her head and opened her amber coloured eyes wide, staring at him. "I'm not coming."

"Why ever not?"

"Because I like it here. They're good to me, and I'm fed the most delicious food, nothing tinned, all the left-overs from the restaurant—bird's nest soup, eggs Foo Yung with prawns, Char Siu roast pork, sour fish, fried crispy duck, you've no idea. And I have a royal blue silk cushion embroidered with pink and white roses to sleep on. I'm staying."

Reilly was astonished. "But don't they shut you in?" he asked. "I saw them!"

"That doesn't bother me, so did Hilda and Bill. And

what's more, absolutely nobody expects me to go hunting."

Reilly was silent. That hurt. Bird's nest soup indeed! The little queen, he thought.

"They call me Lucky," she went on.

He could not think of what to say. "Well, if you really prefer living here as some kind of mascot . . ."

"I don't see what's wrong. I'm learning the Chinese names for everything. It's very interesting. I got rid of my collar so that they wouldn't send me back to Jubilee Road."

"Yeah," said Reilly awkwardly. "Yeah, well, I just came to see if you were okay."

"I'm fine," she said.

Reilly stood up and walked slowly towards the passageway to the main street. His tail was down and his whiskers curved less proudly. "See you some time," he said.

"How do I look?" Dan asked uncertainly, coming into the kitchen. The mouse-brown hair had vanished and been replaced by black. The hair was still short so that it stood up on the crown of his head, but it was softer, like a thick pelt of black fur. He bent to run his hand along Hitachi's back where he lay stretched out by the radiator. Jane looked at her younger brother critically.

"It's okay," she said, walking round him, "but there are one or two bits at the back which are patchy. Didn't you look in the mirror?"

"Oh Hell." Dan stood up, shifting anxiously from foot to foot, and glancing up at the clock. "I'm late already."

"No, no," said Jane, "it's fine. Go as you are, they always turn the lights low at parties, no one will notice. I'll help you do it again some time, it just needs another go."

Dan peered at himself sideways in the hall mirror, trying to see where he had missed. Ludo wandered past on his way to the kitchen.

88

. "Go on, don't worry about it," said Jane. "And I'll look after the cats." Dan reached for his jacket. "Have a good party!" she shouted after him as he swung out of the house, his boots thumping down the steps.

14

Well after midnight on the following night Reilly was out in the graveyard, hunting, when it started to rain. He was behind one of the monuments when he felt the first heavy drops on his back, and heard the steadily increasing patter coming through the ash leaves overhead. He dodged across the alley and was making for home along the top of the wall when he remembered that the cat-flap at Number Eight would be wedged shut. There was only one entrance available at this time of night.

He doubled back and ran along the wall down to Number

Four. Softly he stepped across the gravel in the back yard and lifted the flap with his nose. He slid through. In the Goodings' kitchen Hitachi raised his head and tried to draw himself to a sitting position, but Reilly ignored him and padded past. Hitachi no longer bothered him; he was not a threat.

Reilly was in search of somewhere comfortable to rest. He passed Dan's closed door and glided up the stairs. He entered the living room, where by the light of the street lamp outside he saw Ludo, curled up in a ball at the far end of the sofa.

Some slight sound he made disturbed the little cat, and on the instant he jumped to his feet, all his fur on end, his tail erect and bristling, his ears back. The shock and terror of this sudden apparition in the very inmost sanctum of his home made his heart beat like a hammer and gave him a desperate courage. He advanced sideways towards Reilly, giving a high sing-song warning.

This would be easy, thought Reilly, the little fellow was two thirds his size. Still, you had to give him his due, he was brave. Reilly moved in slowly, face on, his own ears flat, head drawn back into his shoulders, swinging each paw forward to place it dead centre on the line of advance, freeing the other for the first lunging strike.

Ludo backed towards the grate. The fire had long since gone out and only a dull warmth still came from it. Reilly began a loud war chant and moved in for the attack.

On the ground floor directly below, Dan woke. Struggling out of deep sleep he registered the sound of a cat fight, flung himself out of bed and, yanking up his pyjama trousers, hurried to the kitchen to protect Hitachi. But Hitachi was blinking on his blanket in the sudden light. There was no other cat in the room.

Dan paused to listen. Yes, there it was again, that dreadful yowling. It seemed to be coming from behind him. Dan ran out into the yard and tiptoed through the rain on chilled bare feet over the painful gravel to look there. Nothing.

He came back into the kitchen and then realised with stunned surprise that the sound was inside and upstairs.

Good grief, he thought, were there no limits to what the fiend would do? He raced up the stairs two at a time and panted into the sitting room. There was an ear-splitting crescendo of spitting and miauling and in the blaze of light with which Dan filled the room he saw Ludo and Reilly circling slowly round the coffee table.

"Get out!" shouted Dan, and he moved forwards towards Reilly, seizing a cushion off the sofa and making a fierce swipe. Reilly dodged. Then Dan took a second cushion in the other hand, and, holding both low before him, advanced towards the black and white cat, hoping to trap him between the table and the fire. Reilly, cornered, put his ears back and went for Dan's bare ankle with a quick sideways bite.

Dan gave a yell of pain, but he had been taken off guard and he staggered back long enough for Reilly to dash past, out of the door and down the stairs.

Dan went down after him at breakneck speed but it was still not fast enough. Reilly was out through the cat-flap before he could catch him. Dan nursed his bitten ankle,

filling the green plastic bowl with cold water and bathing it until the blood stopped flowing.

He sat down on the floor beside Hitachi. "What are we going to do?" he wondered aloud. Looking at the green basin, he had an idea. He refilled it, pulled it across the floor and pushed it up against the door just below the cat-flap. "There!" he said. Hitachi watched him without moving. "Maybe that'll give black and whitey a nasty surprise. Our cats'll have seen it before they go out." That is, he thought unhappily, if Hitachi's ever well enough to use the cat-flap again . . . He suppressed the thought, padded through to his room and lay down again, hoping to sleep.

His ankle hurt, and he knew he ought to have checked that Ludo had not been scratched, but tomorrow there was the newspaper round and there were only a few hours till he had to get up. He rolled the duvet round himself and closed his eyes purposefully.

The following morning Dan overslept. At his school his form teacher read down the register as far as his name. There was a pause, and she looked up. "Where's Daniel?"

"He's late, Miss. I just saw him coming across the playground," said one of the class.

The door burst open and Dan appeared, red in the face and breathless, hurled his bag down beside his desk and slid into his seat. Miss Crabtree noticed the newly blackened hair, but she decided against comment. It was, just, within the school rules. No green, no pink, no multicolours, only variations of colours natural to hair.

"And what happened to you?"

"Sorry, Miss Crabtree, I overslept."

"All right. Don't let it happen again."

That afternoon when Dan reached home Jane was already back, and greeted him in the hall. "Oh dear, your Mr Patel has been on the phone asking what happened to you this morning. He said one customer had rung up and cancelled her order completely, and he said if it happens again he will have to look for another boy."

"I bet it was Mrs Savage," said Dan grimly. "But how's Hitachi? And is Ludo alright?" and he walked past her into the kitchen.

"Dan, go and *see* Mr Patel, say you're sorry. Or ring him," said Jane.

"Okay, okay, okay," said Dan. "Give me a chance." He took Hitachi's face in his two hands, tilted it gently upwards and looked into his eyes. The old cat shifted slightly in recognition of his touch, but it did not seem to Dan that he could see. He said urgently "When's Mum back? We'd better try and put in the drops without her."

All that week Ludo crept about the house as if in terror for his life. The mere sound of the wind making the cat-flap swing out from its frame and bang back again was enough to start him trembling, and nothing would make him venture out into the garden through it.

He began to make messes in the kitchen and in the hall. Dan tried to avert his mother's anger by cleaning up before she should see, but he was no expert and Mrs Gooding became extremely short-tempered trying to finish off his efforts, scrubbing away with carpet-shampoo at the stains by the front door. The lingering smell filled the house.

On Thursday afternoon there came the final disaster. Although they had made another visit to the vet, Hitachi died. Dan was in the kitchen making a cup of tea on his return from school when the old cat suddenly stood up, gave a wailing cry, walked towards him and then keeled over sideways, his legs doubled up under him at an unnatural angle. Dan knelt beside him, but his eyes gazed unseeing at the wall, and when Dan put a hand on his ribs his heart had stopped beating.

Dan was beside himself with mingled grief and anger at the animal who had been the cause.

When his mother arrived home he was shut in his room with the tape-recorder on. He had laid Hitachi on his side in the kitchen, and had put the piece of blanket over him. Mrs Gooding knocked on Dan's door.

"Dan," she called out, "let me in, I've just seen Hitachi."

Dan opened the door. A thin wisp of cigarette smoke hung in the air, "Oh Dan," she began reproachfully, but when she saw his face she decided to say no more about it. She tried to put an arm round him, but he pushed her away gruffly. His eyes were red.

"I was in there," he said, distress distorting his voice. "He tried to come towards me—Oh Mum, I wish I could have done something."

"You couldn't. Dan, we did everything we could."

"It's all that bloody cat's fault," said Dan viciously. "*Why* couldn't they control him?"

"We did our best," said his mother. "The Braithwaites said they couldn't keep him in, it was bedlam with the others . . . Dan, Hitachi *was* fifteen. He was an old cat when we got Ludo, we knew he wouldn't last for ever."

"He was older than me," said Dan. "For me he was for ever. It won't be home without him. We shouldn't ever have got Ludo, he got left out, oh, and I was so *unkind* to him about that dish. Is it legal for a cat to come into other people's houses and kill their pets? Can't we report it, get him put down or shut away?"

"I don't know. I don't think cats are like dogs, the law doesn't apply in the same way. . ." She sighed, and pushed her hair back out of her eyes. "Anyway it's a bit late now, Hitachi's dead."

"*Mum*," said Dan, "you don't stand up to people. You can't just *let* Hitachi be murdered. Go and give the Braithwaites what for."

"Oh lovie," said Rose Gooding, her eyes filling with tears.

"Sorry," mumbled Dan. "I didn't mean it. It's just— don't cry, Mum, please."

Mrs Gooding sat down on his bed. She blew her nose. Dan put an arm round her, and she smiled ruefully and said "I was supposed to be comforting *you*."

"It's okay, Mum."

"It's not really murder, Dan, you can't say that. Cats aren't people. As far as the black and white cat knows, he's just doing what a cat does, fighting other males for supremacy and taking food where he can get it. They only fight to win, not to kill—the fact that Hitachi died was an accident in a way. And he was quite a fighter in his day, you know."

"Yeah," said Dan. "I suppose we can be quite proud of him. After all, he didn't run away."

Later that evening Dan cheered up a little. He told his mother and sisters about his bowl idea. Reilly had not been near Number Four for several nights. Perhaps, said Dan, he had been scared off after stepping in the bowl.

96

"And I never heard any more from Mrs Savage about Ludo and the smell on her front porch," said Mrs Gooding thoughtfully. "I'll bet that was the werewolf from Number Eight as well."

15

The following Saturday was Daniel's birthday. Dan spent the latter part of the afternoon re-dying his hair with Jane's help.

"Oh Dan!" said Mrs Gooding in exasperation when he emerged. "You haven't had a bowl of dye in your room! What about the carpet?"

"Sorry, Mum," said Dan cheerfully. "Don't think we spilt any. Looks good, hey?"

"Very nice. But I still think you're a little young—"

"Oh Ma, don't be like that," said Jane. "It's his birthday."

Dan carried the bowl of dye through to the kitchen. The bell rang and he dumped it hastily on the settle and hurried back. It was Jonathan, also capped with an inky black mop, Mrs Gooding observed. Jane ran upstairs to change, and Dan led Jonathan through to his room to show him his birthday presents. Mrs Gooding glanced in after them. She saw every surface submerged as if by a tidal wave, leaving dirty clothes, wrapping paper, birthday cards, shoes, books, cushions, records, tape-boxes, empty coffee mugs, even a riffled-through pile of clean and ironed garments. In the middle of the crumpled bed on the floor lay Ludo, fast asleep.

"Tidy it, Dan," called Mrs Gooding after him, "and don't leave Ludo in there, he might have an accident while we're out. Put him in the kitchen."

Dan began half-heartedly tossing things into a heap. He gathered up Ludo and carried him down the hall, rubbing his chin against the top of the little cat's head. When he reached the kitchen he held him out facing him at arm's

length. "Now, I'm leaving you in charge," he said. "If that black and white rotter comes in, it's all up to you. But don't worry, I think we've put him off."

He lowered him to the centre of the floor and went back. Anna and Jonathan and Mrs Gooding were waiting just inside the front door. "Come on, Jane," shouted Mrs Gooding up the stairs. Jane came pounding down.

They left the house, and walked down Jubilee Road and along the main street to the Jade Garden. Inside the restaurant they were led to a table at the far end of the long room, and handed the big six-page menus. One of the waiters stood beside Mrs Gooding's chair, his pencil poised over his notepad.

Dan looked down the long lists; there seemed to be over a hundred dishes to choose from. He hesitated. "I suppose we can't have 'Aromatic Crispy Peking Duck'?" he said longingly, looking at the price.

"Not really," said Mrs Gooding. "Better stick with the set menus, I think. What would you like? Chop suey, sweet and sour pork, boiled rice?" She ordered a bottle of wine.

A fluffy ginger cat wandered into the room from the door behind them and stood in the middle of the restaurant. "Puss, puss," called Dan, swinging round towards it and holding out his hand. He stroked its head.

"Concentrate!" said Mrs Gooding.

Dan gave a sudden exclamation. "It's the Savage's cat! I'm sure it is. Hey, Ginger Rogers?"

The cat looked up at him with amber eyes. The waiter called something over his shoulder towards the kitchen, and a small boy came through the door. He hurried forward and picked up the cat, which purred loudly in his arms, snuggling its face into the crook of his elbow.

"Isn't that the Savage's cat?" persisted Dan to his mother and sisters.

"If it is, she's doing all right here," said Jane, watching as the small boy put the cat down and went back into the kitchen with it trotting eagerly at his heels. The waiter brought the wine and once again stood waiting patiently.

"Oh, that's wonderful," said Dan, and he began to laugh. Jane and Anna and even Mrs Gooding smiled, while Dan shook with glee. Jonathan looked from one to the other, baffled. "I'll explain later," snorted Dan. "Remember what she was on about, when we were going to cricket practice?"

His mother put together an order, and the Chinese waiter went away. Mrs Gooding poured the wine into their glasses and leant across the table. "Happy Birthday, Dan," she said, raising her glass, when Dan's face froze. He was looking at the door behind her.

"Holy cow, look who's just come in."

Mrs Gooding turned to see Hilda Savage walking down the restaurant towards them. "Hallo." She waved. "I saw you all go in and I just wanted to have a word . . ."

"No," breathed Dan. "*Not* on my birthday. I don't know how she has the nerve to show her face in here."

At that instant the fluffy ginger cat came into the room again from the kitchen. Please God, thought Dan, don't let her see it.

But Mrs Savage's glance had fallen on the cat. She stared at it and then said sharply "That's very like Ginger Rogers." She came nearer and peered through the dim light.

Dan saw the small Chinese boy's face framed in the half-open kitchen door. His eyes were wide with alarm, and he caught hold of the edge of the door and held on tight. Dan cleared his throat, and the cat turned her head towards him. Dan made a sudden decision and said "No, that's not your cat, Mrs Savage. We've been here before and that cat has always been here."

"No we haven't . . ." began Anna. Dan kicked her under the table.

"Oh well." Mrs Savage shrugged.

Rose Gooding stood up, took Mrs Savage's arm and

walked her to the door into the main street. "If there's something we should talk about, then it will have to wait, I'm afraid, until tomorrow. This is my son's birthday treat and I really can't discuss anything now—maybe I'll come across to your house tomorrow."

Mrs Savage said, surprised to find herself stepping through the doorway, "All right. I was only going to tell you that we've had a very good offer for our house and—"

"Tomorrow," repeated Mrs Gooding firmly, and she closed the restaurant door.

"Ma, you were wonderful," said Jane. "Whatever got into you?"

Mrs Gooding was flushed as she sat down again. "I've had about enough."

The waiter came in with their order, went out again and then came back to their table. He bowed and smiled. The little boy was at his elbow.

"In your honour," he said. "The owner he wish to say. . ." he paused, stuck for the right words, and the little boy said in a loud whisper "For birthday."

He disappeared for a few minutes, and then came back bearing a large flat blue and white dish from which came a wonderful aroma.

"Peking Duck!" he said, placing the crisply roasted bird on the table in front of Dan and nodded again. Then he leaned over and began to shred up the meat with a fork. The small boy placed beside it a bamboo basket of tiny, pale, thin pancakes, ran back to the kitchen and reappeared with three bowls containing diced cucumber, spring onion and a rich-looking dark sauce. Then they both stood back, smiling. "For you," said the little boy.

"Oh wow!" said Daniel.

Inside Number Four, Jubilee Road, Ludo, left in the kitchen, finished off the saucer of food and curled up to sleep at the far end of the settle, in the corner by the wall, out of

the draughts. He tucked his nose under his black paws and curled small. He missed the comforting warmth of Hitachi.

The Goodings had been gone for over an hour when the cat-flap swung sharply outwards and Reilly was in the room. To begin with he did not see Ludo, and went to inspect the saucers, but Ludo saw him.

The little cat took a sharp breath and his heart began to pound. He stood up and his fur went up on end. In one sudden movement he jumped down from the settle and ran at Reilly, making a quick slash at his flank before the larger cat spun round and answered with two furious glancing blows.

One of them struck Ludo's ear and the other cut him down the side of his shoulder. The two cats engaged in a grappling scuffle on their sides, their front paws clasped round each other, their back legs slashing furiously. With his superior strength Reilly held Ludo pinned down, but Ludo's back claws raked his belly.

Reilly released his grip and jumped upright on to all four feet, hoping to get a purchase with his teeth on the other cat's throat. As he let go, Ludo skidded sideways on the lino floor, and Reilly missed.

Ludo was on his feet again in a second. He had the advantage of knowing the layout of the kitchen by heart. He backed towards the kitchen table, then spun round and leapt on to it, narrowly avoiding the pile of ironing on the top. Reilly, taken by surprise, followed, but as he landed on the table Ludo was waiting for him with a left and right to his face.

Reilly's ear was torn and bleeding, but nothing would stop him now. He leapt on the little cat and rolled him over again on his back.

With a supreme effort Ludo twisted on to his side, and in so doing fell heavily from the edge of the kitchen table on to the seat of the settle. It was lucky for him that he did so, or Reilly would have closed in for a final bite.

Ludo regained his feet, hurled himself to the far end of the settle by the window and scrabbled frantically up the curtains as high as he could go, clinging spread-eagled across the window. Reilly was not going to let him escape. He leapt after him, seizing him round the neck with his paws and closing with his teeth on the back of his neck.

There was a rending sound from the curtains and both cats fell with a thump on to the table, rolling over and over. The pile of ironing was knocked to the floor, scattering right and left.

Nearer and nearer to the table edge by the settle they came, fighting and biting and scratching, oblivious of everything except each other. Suddenly there was a splash and Ludo found himself alone on the table top. Reilly had gone over the edge into the bowl on the settle.

The cold water was a shock to him and he had no idea what had happened. He snorted the liquid out of his nose and mouth, lying on his side and gasping for breath, then he twisted himself upright and stood in utter amazement with all four feet in the bowl.

Ludo took advantage, and from the height of the table made a final scimitar slash to Reilly's face.

Reilly fled.

He leapt down from the bowl, tipping it sideways to the floor, shot across the kitchen to the cat-flap, out through it, up on to the back wall and over to take refuge in the graveyard.

A while later the key turned in the lock and the front door of Number Four swung wide. Mrs Gooding walked in and continued down the hall, followed by Daniel, Jane and Anna. She opened the kitchen door. Behind her Dan was saying, "That was great, thanks, Mum."

She switched on the light. The curtain was ripped in a foot-long tear and spattered with blood. The dye bowl lay upturned, black splashes half across the floor and a black pool immediately round it. Clean ironing lay scattered all about, two white shirts of Dan's blotched and spotted with black stains, a yellow blouse covered in blood. Spots of blood led dramatically towards the cat-flap. Ludo was sitting on the far corner of the settle by the window, his fur still ruffled and ragged-looking.

"Holy cow! This must have been some fight!" said Dan.

"No black and white cat," said Jane. "Ludo must've won."

"Our hero," said Dan, pulling aside the table and going to gather Ludo in his arms, but the little cat was still so alarmed that he spat and cowered against the settle. "It's all right," said Dan soothingly, "in a minute, it's okay, all over now," and he backed away, realising his mistake.

"Oh glory, look at the floor," said Mrs Gooding. "D'you think it'll ever come off?"

"Oh shush, Mum," said Dan. "Ludo's alive and all right, and the black and white cat's gone, that's what matters. I don't care a bit about the shirts, and we'll cover the floor with a mat. I don't know how he did it, but Ludo's won, that's for sure. From now on we can all sleep through the nights in peace."

In the graveyard Reilly opened his eyes, stretched and winced with pain. Every limb ached, and his torn ear was hurting unbearably. He jumped stiffly down from the monument in the early morning light, and walked through the long grass heavy with dew towards the alley.

At the far end, down by the main street, he could see Doreen Bayliss approaching, dressed in a coat and hat, her husband at her side. They were on their way back from church, from the early service.

Reilly walked towards her, sure of an affectionate welcome as usual. He was not altogether wrong.

"Hallo," she said, bending to stroke his back. "Another stray! Look, dear, a black one this time, with a torn ear." She ran a hand down his tail, stood up and walked on.

Reilly trotted after her. "There are an awful lot of strays around here," she was saying. "First Snooky, and now this one. I think I'll ring the R.S.P.C.A. and try and get them to do something about it—maybe they'll be able to find something suitable for Snooky as well."

At the sound of that word, ar-ess-pee-cee-ay, every hair on Reilly's back rose. That terrifying word again! He had not heard it since the previous summer, but how could he ever forget it? When he was a kitten, when there had been that dreadful quarrel and they had talked about drowning him and all the others, someone had shouted then "What about the ar-ess-pee-cee-ay?" It must be the name for some even more dreadful form of death, Reilly was sure. *Some-*

thing suitable for Snooky. What kind of terrible fate had she in mind?

Without pausing to question why she had failed to know him—humans could be very surprising in their behaviour at times—Reilly turned and limped down as fast as he could towards Number Eight.

With some difficulty he scrambled back up on to the wall and manoeuvred himself down into the back yard. He stepped through the cat-flap. Both white cats were lying in the armchair in the kitchen.

"Ho, ho, look at us!" said Bella.

"You can't fool me, I know who you are," said Blanche.

"Black is beautiful, I suppose," said Bella.

Reilly was taken aback. Now for the first time he looked down at his paws. They were black. He examined his chest and underparts. Black as night. For some unfathomable reason he had turned black from head to toe since the previous day.

He stood uncertainly in the middle of the floor. There was no food left in the saucers by the fireplace, but there was half an inch of milk still in one of the bowls.

He went over to it and drank eagerly; there was an extraordinarily unpleasant taste in his mouth, he realised— had been all night. The milk tasted sweet and reassuring.

Blanche gave a loud *miaow*. "Miss Betty, Miss Joyce!" she shouted. "Come quick and look!"

Behind him Reilly could hear Miss Joyce's firm footsteps coming down the hall passage. She opened the door and Reilly turned towards her, crouching low to the floor and looking imploringly up into her face. He moved cautiously towards her, then straightened and rubbed himself against her ankles, going into his customary performance of small rasping mews.

"Good gracious me, not *another* stray," said Miss Joyce. "We've had quite enough trouble with Tiger. No sir, off with you, you'll get nothing from us."

Reilly felt two strong hands go under his soft belly, still tender with scratches, and he was lifted into the air and carried through the door into the back yard. Miss Joyce stepped to the wall, swung him high and the next moment he found himself dropped to the far side, down, down on to the hard paving of the alleyway.

He landed heavily on all four paws, made clumsy by surprise. The pads smarted, his ear ached and throbbed, his limbs were stiff and bruised, and above all he needed food and a place to lie up and recover. He retreated into the long grass under one of the ash trees and began to lick one paw and then another, anxious to regain his normal colouring.

All that day and the next night he lay there, his head throbbing and his body aching and sore. When at last on the following day Reilly felt able to haul himself up to a sitting position and look about, the sun was high overhead, and the harsh light hit his aching eyes like a blow. All that it showed him was the brilliant green of the graveyard, dappled with deep shadow, now no longer truly his. A black wave of despair went over him and he shut out the sight. It had all gone, he thought bitterly, resting his chin on his paws, everything lost, all his hopes and plans. And I thought I'd got it made, he said to himself. What was there left? He hadn't even got his looks any more, and he opened his eyes in disbelief to check yet again the soot-colour of his paws. He wasn't even his own self.

He licked at one paw and with an automatic reflex took in, out of the corner of his eye, a movement in the grass. It came nearer, the stems parted and Francesca's small pointed face appeared.

She regarded him. "Reilly?"

"Yeah."

"I wasn't sure it was you. What on earth have you done to yourself?"

"Oh, nothing much. I'll tell you some other time."

She looked at him wonderingly. He had turned his head away, and the paw he had been licking remained stubbornly black.

"Are you going to stay here?" she asked. "You don't look too good to me."

"I'm all right. But I can't go back to Number Eight— they've thrown me out."

"Oh," said Francesca. She came closer, and lay down in the grass not far from him. He gave her a quick look. She was obviously thinking.

Then she said, "What are you going to live on? How are you going to eat?"

"I'll get by," said Reilly. Something of his old spirit came back to him, and he had a thought. "Hey, what about those blackbird fledglings? Would you like to have a go, later this afternoon?"

Francesca swallowed. There was a long silence.

"Come on," said Reilly. "How about it?"

"Oh dear," said Francesca. "I'm afraid I caught them."

She lowered her head, ears slightly flattened, uncertain how he would take this.

"Oh no."

"It was easy. They were hopping through the undergrowth, they couldn't fly."

"What, *all* of them?" wailed Reilly, giving way and letting his disappointment show. They'd been *his* fledglings, he'd been saving them, and now she'd nicked them from under his very nose. He sat up, his tail twitching with indignation.

"There were only three," said Fran. "Sorry."

You had to admire her nerve, Reilly thought. Aloud he said, "Okay, kid, forget it. No hard feelings."

He sat still for a minute, watching her, and then made a sudden decision. "I've had Jubilee Road, I'm leaving. I think I'll try my luck further up the hill. Fancy coming?"

Fran gave him a long steady look. "For a bit," she said, "maybe. Hold still." She moved closer and began to lick his battered face with brisk, thorough movements. Tenderly her tongue slid over his forehead and cleaned his torn ear. Reilly winced but relaxed again as the licking continued down over his nose; he lifted his head and her tongue caressed his chin and throat, moving down towards his chest.

Reilly closed his eyes and started to hum under his breath, a song, a rhythmic song—for Francesca, for spring and the dead blackbirds, for Hitachi and the brave little black tom. Louder and louder he sang, his throat rumbling and throbbing, a song of farewell to Jubilee Road and a song of hope for the life of Reilly yet to come. Anyone listening would have said that he was purring.